people & project management

by Rob Thomsett
Preface by Edward Yourdon
Illustrations by George Armstrong

Yourdon Press
1133 Avenue of the Americas
New York, New York 10036

Library of Congress Cataloging in Publication Data

Thomsett, Rob.
     People and project management.

     Bibliography: p.

     1. Electronic data processing--Management.
I. Title.
QA76.9.M3T49   658'.05   80-51921
ISBN 0-917072-21-9

Printed in the United States of America

Library of Congress Catalog Number 80-51921

ISBN: 0-917072-21-9

This book was set in Times Roman by YOURDON Press,
1133 Avenue of the Americas, New York, N.Y., using a
PDP-11/45 running under the UNIX[†] operating system.

[†]UNIX is a registered trademark of Bell Laboratories.

Thanks

To the Yourdon Press editorial team
for providing invaluable advice and assistance
To Phil Hutson for inspiring the drawings that begin each chapter
To Dennis Davie for giving me the chance
To Ed Yourdon, Larry Constantine, and Jerry Weinberg
for reminding us that people still exist in computing
To Peter, Ann, and Camille for being who you are

Warning

Much of the material in this book could be considered radical by your organization. When you and the other team members have finished with it, drop it into your manager's in-tray (assuming, of course, that there is room).

Contents

Acknowledgments

During the past six years, I have worked exclusively as one member of an education/consulting team. I worked with Peter Lonsdale for the first five years and have worked with Ann Bromwich for the past year (with Peter dropping in from time to time). This book is about what we learned together as a team, what we learned from others, and what we learned from each other. Our success as a team that evolved and grew stronger provided us with the knowledge and confidence that teams do work and work *better*. *I* have written down some of what *we* learned, but *we* learned together.

Reprint Permissions

We thank the following organizations for their permission to reprint certain of the diagrams appearing in this book. Listed in order of their appearance in this text, the diagrams and acknowledgments are

Figure 2.2. **A working distributed-control system.** From *Designing*
(p. 21) *Freedom,* by Stafford Beer (Chichester, England: John Wiley & Sons, Ltd., 1974), p. 83. Copyright © 1974 by Stafford Beer. Adapted and reprinted by permission.

Figure 2.3. **Shannon and Weaver's model of communication.** From
(p. 22) *The Mathematical Theory of Communication,* 1st ed., by C.E. Shannon and W. Weaver, p. 98. Copyright © 1949 by the University of Illinois Press, Urbana, Ill. Copyright renewed in 1977. Reprinted by permission.

Figure 3.3. **Factors influencing behavior.** From *Organization and*
(p. 37) *Management: A Systems and Contingency Approach,* 3rd ed., by F.E. Kast and J.E. Rosenzweig, p. 241. Copyright © 1979 by McGraw-Hill, Inc. Adapted and used with the permission of the McGraw-Hill Book Company.

Figure 3.6. **An integrated model including implementation tech-**
(p. 42) **niques.** From "A New Strategy for Job Enrichment," by J.R. Hackman et al. Copyright © 1975 by the Regents of the University of California. Reprinted from *California Management Review,* Vol. 17, No. 4, p. 62, by permission of the Regents.

Figure 4.3. **Second-generation phased model.** From *Programming*
(p. 54) *Project Management Guide,* by P. Metzger, IBM Technical Report No. GA36-0005-1 (Gaithersburg, Md.: July 1974). Copyright © 1974 by International Business Machines Corporation. Reprinted by permission.

Preface

Some ten years ago, Gerald Weinberg wrote a book, *The Psychology of Computer Programming,* which has served ever since as a bible for EDP managers who want to understand the *human* side of the programming business. Now — finally! — we are beginning to see some books that deserve to be placed next to Weinberg's on the bookshelf. Phil Semprevivo's *Teams in Information Systems Development,* published earlier this year by YOURDON Press, is one, and this book by Rob Thomsett is another.

Rob's book is not exclusively devoted to programming teams and walkthroughs; nor is it exclusively concerned with project management, in the classical sense; nor could it be considered a primer on the structured development techniques of structured analysis, structured design, and structured programming. Rather, it is about *all* of these things, and how they fit together in a well-organized project. As Rob points out, one can't really separate the issues of *people* from the issues of systems development techniques and project control tools — they are, as Tom DeMarco would say, deeply intertwingled.

One of the most refreshing things about Rob's book is his emphasis on the system of building systems. All too often, we data processing people concentrate all of our energies on the *computer* system we intend to foist upon some innocent user; we spend far too little time worrying about the larger system that constitutes the user's entire environment. Even worse, we ignore the fact that the project team is *itself* a system, and that it has to interact with the larger system, that is the organization in which the project team works. This can lead to the anomalies that many of us have seen in EDP projects but have never completely understood: projects in which the programmers, rather than the managers, control events; projects in which *nobody* controls anything, despite management's illusion that they are in control; and so on.

People & Project Management won't turn ugly ducklings into swans: It won't make you a project manager if you have no experience or training in the area. But it will give you an enormous amount of food for thought, as well as an extensive bibliography of books and articles that you should read if you feel that your primary job is that of managing people in a technical environment. It will be equally valuable for the programmer/analyst who wonders how best to communicate with management (which usually means more than just the immediate supervisor) and why communication is sometimes impossible.

Rob Thomsett's book may gain more immediate recognition than *The Psychology of Computer Programming* did ten years ago, because Weinberg's book, with its profound effect on the EDP profession, cleared the way for *People & Project Management*. Weinberg once mentioned to me that *The Psychology of Computer Programming* was rejected by the first three publishers to whom he sent the manuscript, on the basis that there were no university courses on the subject. Almost nobody in 1971 understood the significance of the human side of data processing — and, even now, far too few people do. It may well be that *People & Project Management* will become recognized as one of *the* significant books of the 1980s.

November 1980   Edward Yourdon
                                                         New York, New York

Foreword

Ours is a world of paradoxes. For the past five years, our research team has spent nearly one thousand hours with hundreds of computer people and users in attempting to resolve one of the most frustrating and fundamental paradoxes: How is it that competent computer professionals working with the most advanced technology continue to develop computer systems that don't work, exceed cost estimates, and fall behind schedule?

We have realized that part of the resolution of this paradox is that computer people *are* professional and that they *are* working with advanced technology. As researchers, we have grown increasingly aware that another part of the answer to the paradox is the dichotomy between knowing the problem and yet not being able to do something about it. We know that the communications barrier between users and computer people is an important piece of the problem. We also have learned that some of the answer lies with the managers, the complexity of systems, and organization structure. The more we have learned about the paradox of project management, the more complex the paradox has appeared to us.

Of course, as we were coming to the realization that the more we studied the subject the more complex the subject seemed, we ourselves were observing and experiencing a system behavior that is well known to all wise systems people: As we broadened the problem boundary, the problem grew more complex.

In looking at the possible resolution of this paradox, we were very conscious that prevailing approaches and texts examining this area were highly prescriptive: "If you use this technique, and these forms, . . . then . . . success!" We concluded from discussion and observation that the "cookbook" approach simply didn't work, or at best didn't work consistently. A technique that proved successful in one project proved totally useless in another, even within the same organization.

As a result, in our own seminars and project work, we have attempted to avoid prescriptive answers. Instead, we have tried to distill a high-level set of systematic guidelines that could be used by members of a project to evaluate control and management issues within their particular organizations, and to facilitate the design and implementation of project management systems that work.

In the process of learning about and integrating this broad set of guidelines, we became convinced that we had discovered some answers that actually *worked* in the real world. We also became convinced that all of the project approaches available commercially or outlined in classic texts were incomplete; and as teams using our guidelines began to work together better and to meet deadlines, we found it increasingly hard to remain completely non-prescriptive. Therefore, you will find that we are guilty of providing prescriptive answers in some instances.

What you have then in this short book is a summary of our learning and our guidelines for developing successful project management systems that treat computer people as people. The book is brief because the guidelines are simple — their simplicity appears intuitively correct, as it seems all good design is simple. It's brief, too, because we suspect that project people are not allowed time to read about their work — the better you are, the more projects you work on (computing's version of Catch 22).

We hope that you will use and enjoy this book, and that it helps you to make your dreams come true on time.

November 1980   Rob Thomsett
                                                                   Sydney, Australia

Overview

What this book is about is people. It is about people who are involved in the management of the analysis, design, implementation, and maintenance of computer systems that are used by other people to do their work. It is about the information that all people involved in computer projects need in order to understand both the process and the progress within the process. It is about designing systems to enable the free flow of project information between people. It is about techniques that can assure that projects remain in control. Most importantly, it is about people . . . people working together to achieve a common goal of developing projects on time and within budget.

Traditional approaches to project management separate people issues from the functions and techniques of project management. At best, they include a "potted" summary of the research on motivation by Maslow [1] and Herzberg [2]; a brief discussion of project teams, especially IBM's chief programmer concept [3]; and some ideas on the role of leaders. What we are saying in this book is that it is *people* who use the tools; who make decisions; who plan, schedule, and review project performance; who use the structured methodologies to develop systems; who are responsible for projects; and who communicate with other people about what is going on. *People, not project management systems, manage systems.*

Aron recognized the critical issue of people and management when he commented on a study of more than a dozen project disasters:

> "We ran into problems because we didn't know how to manage what we had, not because we lacked the techniques themselves."*

---

*J.D. Aron, "The 'Super-programmer Project'," *Software Engineering Techniques: Report on the 1969 Rome Conference,* J.N. Buxton and B. Randell, eds. (Brussels, Belgium: NATO Science Committee, 1970), p. 52. Keider [4] details another study of project failures and provides a comprehensive set of reasons for those failures, the majority of which can be attributed to people problems.

The structure of this book reflects this primary concern with people: Chapter 1 discusses systems and recently developed systems laws that can provide people with a framework for coping with the uncertainty and complexity of systems with which they have to work. Chapter 2 on control and information explores what have emerged as the *fundamental* issues in project management: What is control? What is information? How do these concepts relate to each other?

Chapter 3 examines recent developments in the areas of individual motivation, job satisfaction, performance, and attitudes toward work. It focuses on teams with an emphasis on leadership roles and management issues. In Chapter 4, we consider contemporary developments in systems development methodologies and in software engineering concepts. Using the material in the first three chapters, we evaluate the impact of these methodologies on the control of the systems life-cycle.

In Chapter 5, we survey the processes of project planning, work definition, tracking, and reporting. In the sixth chapter, we examine a set of broad guidelines for project management systems that integrate the processes and people-management techniques, which have been proved to work in the real world. Finally, in Chapter 7, we look at possible approaches to solving the problems of getting your system to work in your organization.

At the end of each of Chapters 1 to 6, we have included a game or simulation exercise that highlights some of the significant points in the chapter. All of the team exercises in this book are designed to mirror the real world of projects and some of the issues raised in each chapter. What happens in the exercises is similar to what happens in projects, in that results vary depending on the people who participate in them. Rather than tell you what results you should look for, we think part of the exercises' usefulness is in your learning to observe and to draw your own conclusions in the discussions that should follow each of the exercises. We suggest that your team play these games, preferably during work hours. Depending on your management's opinion of laughter and learning, lunch-times and coffee breaks may be used as suitable alternatives.

We hope that you will start reading this brief book with Chapter 1 and read all the way to the end. You may be tempted to peek at Chapters 6 and 7 first to see what it's all leading up to, but, as with all journeys, the best part is usually the process of getting there. If you do read Chapter 6 or 7 first and ask "Is that all?" then drop us a line. You probably have a lot of things you could teach us and we'd undoubtedly make a great team.

Throughout this book, we berate management for not providing enough feedback to teams, and suggest that teams provide much more feedback to managers. So, we would be inconsistent in our theories for action if we didn't ask you to provide feedback to us. Please drop us a line — on the back of the volumes of project control forms and reports you'll no longer need — or on anything. Let us know how the ideas presented in the book work for you, and if there is anything we can do to assist you. Send your comments to Rob Thomsett, in care of

DP Education Pty., Ltd.   **or**   YOURDON Press
9 Hill Street   1133 Avenue of the Americas
Roseville, N.S.W. 2069   New York, N.Y. 10036
Australia   United States of America

We *will* write back and close the feedback loop.

References: Overview

1. A. Maslow, *The Farther Reaches of Human Nature* (New York: Penguin Books, 1971).

2. F. Herzberg, *The Managerial Choice: To Be Efficient and to Be Human* (Homewood, Ill.: Dow Jones-Irwin, 1976).

3. F.T. Baker and H.D. Mills, "Chief Programmer Teams," *Datamation,* Vol. 19, No. 12 (December 1973), pp. 58-61.

4. S.P. Keider, "Why Projects Fail," *Datamation,* Vol. 20, No. 12 (December 1974), pp. 53-55.

1
Systems

The team members dream up a system diagram.

1
Systems

"Shall we take a radio apart to find the voice?"
—Stafford Beer*

The systems approach has been with us since the early 1960s. It grew from the work of theorists and researchers[†] who looked across all sciences to develop a general set of laws that explained the behavior of systems, whether ecological, man-made, philosophical, or societal. As is often the way, this set of laws has now become the property of academics and writers who suffer from a general systems disease that Weinberg calls "hypermathematisis" — reducing the laws to a level so far removed from the real world that most students find them impenetrable and useless [2]. This is unfortunate, as systems theory has produced a set of very powerful laws that can help computer people and users to understand the behavior of systems.

The basic concept of systems theory is that a system exists as a perceivable entity, and that a boundary separates the observed system from its environment. The systems that concern us (computer systems, management systems, project information systems) accept input from their environment, do something to that input according to the particular system's purpose, and ideally produce some different and useful output. To achieve this transformation, systems have components, modules, or subsystems that relate to and communicate with other components. The total complexity of a system is a measure of the internal complexity of the components, the complexity of the relationships between components, and the complexity of its environment. Obviously, if we wish to understand, control, or design a system, we must be able to reproduce its complexity [3, 4]. Constantine and others [5, 6] recognized this requirement in the early 1960s and developed the structured design approach.

---

*S. Beer, *Platform for Change* (New York: John Wiley & Sons, 1975), p. 122.
[†]For excellent discussions of systems thinking, see Emery [1].

Complexity *is* a key issue in project management systems. For many project people — faced with diverse user groups, office politics, a growing number of distinct project roles (those of analysts, database groups, communications experts, programmers, and so on), new technology, and the system's internal complexity — projects are intrinsically more complex than project people individually can understand.

Alexander has stated, "Today more and more design problems are reaching insoluble levels of complexity."* In our work with complex projects and systems, we found that the following observations about systems gave us a framework for understanding their behavior.

■ The whole is more than the sum of the parts

The observation that the whole is more than the sum of the parts is probably the basic tenet of systems theory. Obviously, the system — its boundaries, components, relationships, and goals — is much more than just the sum of its parts. Beer's example of the radio, quoted on the preceding page, illustrates our point: Its individual components are simple. If we lay them out separately on a table, they still remain simple components. However, if we introduce a designed set of relationships between those components (solder, wire, and so on) to form a whole, then when switched on, the whole produces a voice. Change one connection, one component, or take the whole apart, and the voice stops (or does it?).

Our experience with highly successful project teams further substantiates this observation. A well-functioning team has a special "feel" about it: It performs well, produces high quality systems, and is highly creative when faced with complex problems. This "feel" is often called synergy, empathy, or symbiosis (or $2 + 2 = 5$). Break up the team and the individuals' performances can suffer considerably. Not only has this been shown repeatedly to be true in computer project teams, but also members of rock groups such as the Beatles are still trying to match individually the creativity and success that the "whole" once possessed. The relationships between the components and the system's goals are as important as the components themselves.† As any

---

*C. Alexander, *Notes on the Synthesis of Form* (Cambridge, Mass.: Harvard University Press, 1964), p. 3.

†This observation highlights the classic difference between the mechanistic or scientific method of observation (which destroys the system by examining individual components in isolation) and the systemic or organic method (which studies the system as it exists in its environment). The paradox in the scientific approach is neatly stated by Weinberg in his Perfect Systems Law: "True systems properties cannot be investigated." [7]

experienced maintenance programmer will testify, if you change a system's functions or remove one of its modules, you've changed the system itself.

■ What is the whole is a function of who's looking at it

The idea that what is the whole is a function of who is viewing it introduces a real problem: that of defining boundaries between the "whole," or system, and its environment. An architect may regard a house's electrical, heating, and water systems and living-space requirements as one large system. A mechanical engineer may view the heating equipment as a system and the house as its environment, while an environmental designer may view the house and family as a component in a total urban system. The house, its occupants, and its street are the same in each of these cases, but how they fit into a given system depends on the observer. Again, this problem is familiar to systems experts who may start with a small, easily defined system, which may grow bigger and more complex as more users become involved and as its boundaries widen. The problem is compounded by the system's expansion appearing to be rational and sensible. Statements such as "Well, if we just generalize this module, then these other people can use the system as well, and besides, it wouldn't cost much more,"* are danger signs that the analyst or programmer is about to become entangled in the problem of where to draw the system boundaries.

What is being explored in this example is a very perplexing system property: *The boundary of a system is dynamic, or flexible, and where it is drawn is really up to the observer.* In most cases, we believe the boundaries are drawn from an economic, cost-effective, organizational, or resource viewpoint — *not* because that's where they have to be. Given four programmers and three months, the project team might draw the boundaries at point X. With ten programmers and six months, the *same* system might have its boundaries at point Y (see Fig. 1.1, on the following page).†

---

*This comment reflects a version of a classic programmer game called SMOP: The user requests a change, and the programmers agree that it's just a small matter of programming. Of course, SMOP produces another game, LMFM or large matter for maintenance.

†This system property of dynamic, or flexible, boundaries has significant implications for project control, and it is explored in more detail in Chapter 5.

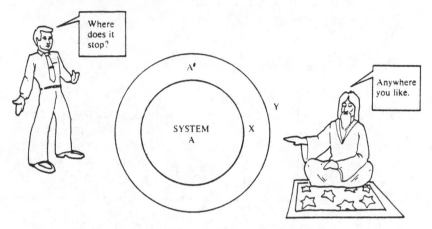

Fig. 1.1. The dynamic nature of boundaries.

■ The relationships between wholes are the problem

A corollary to the previous systems concept is the observation that the relationships between wholes are the problem as it applies to systems and boundaries, taking into account what is euphemistically called "boundary clashes." Since the boundary between a system and its environment is an arbitrary choice and since all systems are a part of other systems, we can state that if the boundaries as decided lead to communication problems between systems, then the *choice of boundaries was incorrect,* as shown in Figs. 1.2 and 1.3.

Fig. 1.2. Boundary clash: incorrect choice.

Fig. 1.3. No boundary clash: correct choice.

In project management terms, the existence of a boundary clash (remember — this is the result of arbitrary choice, not intractable reality) is manifest as conflicts in responsibility, and in delayed, distorted, and confused communication, which in turn result in incorrect estimation, unrealistic deadlines, and inaccurate progress reports. It has taken the computing profession a long, expensive, and painful time to realize that fully integrated teams of users and programmers produce much more trouble-free systems implementations than the prevailing project team approach of separating users from technical people. Therefore, what this crucial observation emphasizes is that

> *The first step in achieving workable project management is to correctly draw the boundaries between the various people systems — users, management, and team — involved in the project and around the business system being developed.*

■ **The whole is a whole because it is**

Many programmers and systems people have become confounded by the belief that the whole can be made up in one way only, as determined by the goals of the system. Gall suggests that, at the highest level of abstraction, there are three distinct categories of goals in any system and that the closer these goals correspond to each other the more predictable is the system's behavior [8]. The goals are

- the stated purpose of the system
- the functions as designed into the system
- the goals of the system itself

The first two goals are well known to analysts and designers. Most systems disasters can be attributed to the difference between what the users wanted (purpose) and what was implemented in the design (function). However, the third goal, which is a significant one ignored by many experienced people, concerns the survival of complex systems — that is, the system's energy or life-force. Any system under threat — a computer system with unexpected user changes, for example, or an organization with a shift in consumer demand or faced with increased government regulation, or a project team with a new team member — will strive within its limits to accommodate the disturbance with a minimum of disruption to its functioning. *Faced with continuing disruptions, the prime goal of systems becomes survival.*

Beer proposes that the proportion of systems effort devoted to the system's survival (totally independent of its stated function's usefulness) grows with time and can be in excess of thirty percent [9]. Brooks' mythical man-month concept is another example of this phenomenon: Adding people to the project ultimately means more project resources are consumed to assure that the team survives as a unit [10].

At a more practical level, all systems people are conscious of the multiplicity of "stated" goals for systems, goals that are often in conflict at different levels of observation and analysis. One of the most common systems development mistakes is to base design on what the managers or manuals say happens at the work place. Unfortunately, faced with a mish-mash of goals and functions and with statements like "Ignore what that person says; this is really what happens here," most systems people have to rely on yet another perceived (and conflicting) goal — the one that *they* perceive as pertaining to the system. A good example of this problem was the statement published by an Australian Parliamentary committee after reviewing a proposed system for its department's manpower procedures: "It is not only a question of whether the system will meet its design goals. Even if it does so in every respect, it has not yet been demonstrated that all the goals are closely matched to the real information needs of managers. . . ."*

In conclusion, these observations about these four aspects of the whole provide us with a framework within which to consider the entire system (people, management, computer, information) in the environment of project control. We can now explore in the next chapter a primary goal that we believe exists for all projects: control.

---

*This example is from the Parliamentary Accounts Committee [11] following its examination of the MANDATA system. The system was commenced in the mid-Sixties to process staff administration functions and to provide for management information needs such as manpower planning. In 1979, it was installed in limited operation. Estimates on resources consumed by the project vary from two- to four-hundred people-years.

TEAM EXERCISE

The Tinkertoy® Game

This exercise examines problems people have when asked to describe a relatively simple model and then in communicating the description to other people. Specifically, it simulates a typical user, analyst, and programmer situation in which the users can visualize their system but need to explain it to the computer people.

O Compose two teams of three to six people. Designate one team the "user" team; the other, the "construction" team (which represents the computer staff).

O Using twenty or so Tinkertoy game pieces, construct a model (anything you can imagine — ours have challenged those out of *Star Wars*).

O Give the construction team Tinkertoy pieces identical to those used in the model.

O Have the user team describe verbally to the construction team how to build the model. (No written messages or any other form of documentation may be used.)

O Allow twenty to thirty minutes for the user team to pass *one-way* messages to the construction team, and another five to ten minutes for the building team to question the describing team (users).

O Have the construction team try to reproduce the model relying only on the descriptions provided to them.

References: Chapter 1

1. F.E. Emery, ed., *Systems Thinking* (Harmondsworth, Middlesex, England: Penguin Books, 1969).

2. G.M. Weinberg, *An Introduction to General Systems Thinking* (New York: John Wiley & Sons, 1975), p. 68.

3. W.R. Ashby, *Introduction to Cybernetics* (New York: John Wiley & Sons, 1961).

4. S. Beer, *Platform for Change* (New York: John Wiley & Sons, 1975), p. 223.

5. W. Stevens, G. Myers, and L. Constantine, "Structured Design," *IBM Systems Journal*, Vol. 13, No. 2 (May 1974), pp. 115-39.

6. E. Yourdon and L.L. Constantine, *Structured Design: Fundamentals of a Discipline of Computer Program and Systems Design* (New York: YOURDON Press, 1978).

7. G.M. Weinberg, op. cit., p. 160.

8. J. Gall, *Systemantics* (New York: Pocket Books, 1978), pp. 88-89.

9. S. Beer, *Designing Freedom* (New York: John Wiley & Sons, 1974), pp. 85-86.

10. F.P. Brooks, Jr., *The Mythical Man-Month* (Reading, Mass.: Addison-Wesley, 1975), pp. 21-26.

11. Joint Committee of Public Accounts, *Use of ADP in Commonwealth Public Sector*, Report 175 (Canberra: Australian Government Publishing Service, 1979), p. 88.

2
Control
and Information

The team members select their tasks.

2
Control
and Information

■ **Project control or programmer control?**

During one project management seminar, we simulated a meeting between a project team and a management review committee. The meeting's purpose was to consider the users' request for a major change and to prevent the project from going out of control. As soon as the meeting began, the programmers took the offensive, informing management that they had heard of the change through the grapevine and had formulated two options for management's consideration: Since the change involved a significant addition to the system's functions, management could either increase the time scheduled for the project and not add people (this group was obviously aware of Brooks' man-month lesson [1]); or drop a less crucial part of the system and keep the deadlines as established during project planning.

Management, of course, was totally flustered (after all, *management* made decisions on the options and then told the programmers what to do!). Management demanded time to think about the situation. The programmers replied that they could not continue work on the system until the choice was made. Management, in an attempt to regain control, told the programmers to work on the documentation in the interim (which the programmers couldn't do because the system had already been completely documented).

■ **The conflict**

What this encounter illustrates are the crucial relationship between control and information and the confusion between the different models of control that exist in most organizations. The important question to ask about the encounter is, "Was the project still in control?'' Obviously, whether it was depended on management's response to the two options presented by the programmers. The choice of *either* option by management would have kept the project under control. Where the confusion existed, as has happened in almost every project we have observed, was in the second "control" system: that of management versus the programmers, or deciding who was master.

The conflict between *project* control and *management* control constitutes the biggest single problem in project management. For instance, the project in our example would have remained in control (in the sense of being a workable, programmable project) independent of the option chosen, yet the interplay between team members and management meant the project had moved toward being out of control. The paradox is that both groups were equally committed to the project's remaining in control, although we must suggest that management's behavior often shows a commitment to the opposite! When we discuss control, then, we must be very specific about which control system we're talking.

■ Project control

Let's leave a discussion of the management control system until Chapter 3 and concentrate for now on the project control system. *Project control can be defined as a state.* Every project can exist in one of two states: in control — that is, within its estimated budgets, deadlines, resources, and user requirements — or out of control.

These two states can be examined by using Ashby's very powerful model of control, modified below to reflect a project team environment in which there are five basic components of control [2].

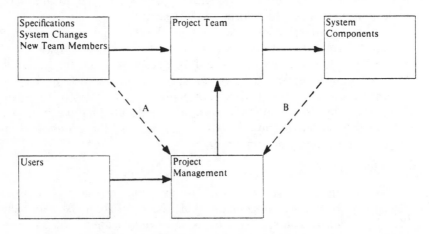

Fig. 2.1. Modification of Ashby's control model.

The model in Fig. 2.1 on the preceding page suggests that the users perform the highest-level function of setting the objectives for the system and for its acceptable performance. These requirements are passed to the project team via management, who regulates the implementation process undertaken by the team. The team transforms the specifications, schedules, and other inputs into the system components. Management uses feedback loop B to check that the output from the team is within the acceptable limits. If the output is acceptable, then the project is in control. If the output differs from the acceptable and agreed-upon limits, the project is out of control.

Management, on the basis of this information, has three choices for action under Ashby's rules: One, it can alter the project team's process, e.g., by adding resources or increasing training; two, it can provide feedback to the users and change the goals of the system to accommodate the variance, e.g., by changing deadlines or by dropping or adding system functions; or three, it can ignore the signals and hope the variance goes away, or tell the team to work harder. The third choice is obviously a pathological version of the second, but is nevertheless very common in computer projects. Choices one and two can restore the project into an in-control state, while the third can perpetuate the out-of-control state.

Another important feature of this control model is that it highlights the "management-by-crisis" syndrome: As in the previous example, actions to bring the system back in control are taken *after* a variance has occurred. If the variance in the system has been caused by a change in specifications rather than a breakdown in the team's operations, then this situation can be prevented by the use of feed-forward loop A. In this case, the impact of the variance can be anticipated prior to its affecting the team, and the first or second choices for action can be implemented *before* the event.

The lines connecting the functions in this model represent communication channels, passing information between the functions.* If any one of these lines is too long, too slow, an inappropriate filter, distortional, or simply nonexistent, then control *cannot* exist in the system. It's really that simple. For the project control system to function, the communication lines must be designed with an appropriate response time and sufficient information-handling capacity. It is these information lines that are the physically manifest forms and reports of project management systems.

---

*Obviously, these channels must be duplex, that is, able to transmit two messages simultaneously in the same or opposite directions.

From Ashby's model, we can derive the second step in developing our working project system:

Project management systems must provide adequate communication channels, capable of passing suitably timed and filtered information between the five basic components of control.

For example, a command "work harder" from management to a project team, elicited in response to information passed from system components to management that the project deadline had slipped, would normally be viewed by the project team as a distorted message. This distortion could cause the slippage information to further degenerate into data* that would elicit the project team's response to management, "We are now working one hundred hours per week on the project, boss." In fact, the team, already working at its limit (eighty hours per week), has been placed in that typical double-bind of reporting the real situation, receiving inadequate or hostile responses, and responding by feeding back data of the kind the team thinks management would like.

Obviously, this scenario could be modified to reflect breakdowns in any of the other channels between components. As an exercise, try to imagine what would happen to control if the channel between users and management were inadequate. (Remember, we are talking here about the project control system, not the management control system.)

Ashby's model raises other relevant questions: Who are the decision-makers? The answer is, of course, the users, the management, and members of the project team. (Note that decision-making is not vested only in the traditional management function.) Where is control? To answer this question, examine a project that is in control: An interesting fact becomes apparent. It's impossible to isolate the single component or person who is keeping the project in control.†

Ashby's model illustrates that control — the component of the system that assures that progress corresponds to the objectives and plans of the original system — is distributed throughout the whole model. If any of the functions (users, management, or team) are not working well or if any of the communication lines (from management to team, team to management, users to management, or output to management) are inadequate or nonexistent, then control cannot exist. A failure in *any* one of these components can lead to the project's moving into an out-of-control state.

---

*Note that we make a distinction here between data as being useless and information as being useful.

†As G.M. and D. Weinberg observed: "Regulation is invisible when it works." [3]

Beer draws an analogy between this control model and the human physiological system [4]: Our thermostatic regulators will adjust our physical systems' temperatures causing us either to shiver when we're cold, or to perspire when we're hot. We cannot isolate this thermostatic function, for it is distributed throughout our nervous system. Beer suggests that all our control systems should be designed according to this distributed model, with a blend of central and peripheral regulatory information (see Fig. 2.2.). The brain, our highest level of control, need not get involved in our thermostatic process unless the acceptable limits of the body's thermostat are exceeded. When the acceptable limits are exceeded, the brain then takes corrective actions — e.g., decides to instruct the body to put on more clothes or to go for a swim — to restore the thermostatic system to an in-control state.

Fig. 2.2. A working distributed-control system.

All viable control systems involve a common set of functions joined by communication channels that pass selectively filtered and amplified information. This enables the traditional processes of planning, evaluating, reviewing, and decision-making to take place in a distributed fashion, and at the appropriate level in the control system. (It would be ridiculous if, for example, we had to stop talking to concentrate on minor body temperature variations.) Having accepted this, we have two additional aspects of control to consider: communication and the difference between data and information.

■ Communication

In our project systems, it is *people* who perform the control processes — for example, by making decisions — and *people* who act as the information channels. Unfortunately, as most analysts might have learned, people are not renowned for their ability to communicate clearly. (How many times have we heard, "Oh! Is *that* what you meant to say!") In an environment in which management has the dual role of project control and programmer control (raises, promotions, and so on), this problem can be complicated by concern about letting management know about project difficulties because the difficulties might reflect badly on the team.

Shannon and Weaver developed a very useful model of communication [5]: For a source (say, a project team) to send information to a destination (users, for instance), the source must be able to encode the message into a suitable form to be passed along the channel; to understand the message, the destination must be able to match the encoding with corresponding decoding. Noise in the channel (caused by, say, jargon, office politics, or personal differences) can distort the message (see Fig. 2.3.).

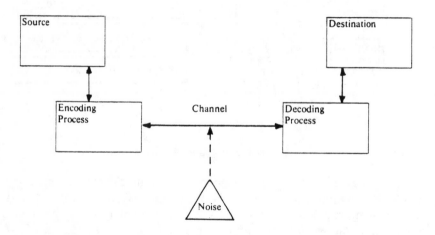

Fig. 2.3. Shannon and Weaver's model of communication.

A malfunction in any of the components of the communication process, be it in encoding, noise in the channel, or in decoding, will lead to a communication breakdown. (Computer engineers, who design hardware and who are aware of this potential for malfunction, use techniques of redundancy, parity-checking, and feedback to ensure that the communication process is successful.) Yet, the number of project control systems that ignore the crucial element of feedback and use only one-way communication channels is very disturbing. Too many programmers have told us that they had not used project control systems properly because they had received inadequate feedback or, in some cases, no feedback at all.

Fig. 2.4a. Communication with feedback.*

Fig. 2.4b. Communication without feedback.

■ Data versus information

The second problem in regard to control is simply recognizing the difference between data and information. Beer differentiated between them by stating, "Data are the very latest kind of pollution. Information is what changes us."[†] We agree with Beer's distinction that information is data that changes us by increasing our understanding of a situation. For example, the string of numbers 28 11 2 17 5 6 14 is data that could have a variety of meanings. Determining whether this data is information and the significance of the information depends on who is looking at it. A mathematician looking at this data might regard it as information relating to a particular series; a sports fan might observe the numbers as cricket scores; or if you had the numbers on a lottery ticket, and they were the winning numbers, you would regard the data as very significant information, no doubt. Of course, if you aren't a mathematician, sports fan, or lottery ticket holder, the numbers would

---

*It's fun to supply your own captions for the situation depicted in Fig. 2.4a: For example, "Great! Now we're only two years behind schedule!"
[†]S. Beer, *Platform for Change* (New York: John Wiley & Sons, 1975), p. 223.

probably be just data to you. Regardless of the particular significance of the data, the information needed in any project to provide control is a *very small set* compared with the total data that exists. Moreover, the required information is identical for the team *and* for management, although management's information is a filtered version of the team's information.*

The design of project control systems must incorporate these basic information requirements and avoid the common approach of data explosion, which is symptomatic of many project management systems. (Some packaged project control methodologies have more than twenty data collection forms!) The fact that the team spent fifty hours on the project in the reporting period is data. That the team members spent fifty hours on the project when they expected to spend eighty hours may be information. The fact that the team spent fifty hours on the project and the project is still in an in-control state is information. The topic of project information will be explored further in Chapter 5 and Chapter 6.

Finally, project control is about people being supported by information systems that enable them to understand the complexity of issues characterizing the project they are attempting to control. Ashby's Law of Requisite Variety [2] states that in order to maintain control, since most systems are more complex than we individually can understand, we must use information either to increase our set of possible actions (increase our variety) or to decrease the set of possible actions of the system (reduce the system's variety).† This law is illustrated in Fig. 2.5, on the following page. Whichever option or blend of options we choose, Ashby's Law is irrevocable: If we don't match a system's variety, the system will eventually go out of control.

Our project control systems must facilitate this matching of variety by transferring information between the components of the control system and by distributing the decision capability to the relevant functions.

---

*This observation is supported by Boehm [6], Lientz and Swanson [7], Walston and Felix [8], and others working in the field of software metrics (see Chapter 5). It is also supported by the work of Canning [9], and of Rockart [10], who has developed a system of critical success factors that examines the basic information requirements of organizations.

†Variety is Ashby's measurement of complexity and represents the possible number of states, modes, or actions that a system is capable of adopting or taking. For example, the variety of an electric light is two (on or off), unless, of course, it's broken, a situation that could be defined as a third state.

a. Requirement for the system.

b. Actual behavior of the system.

**c. Solution 1: Increase variety
   of controller.**

d. Solution 2: Reduce system variety.

Fig. 2.5. Ashby's Law of Requisite Variety.

■ **Summary**

In Chapters 1 and 2, we have introduced fundamental issues that must be resolved prior to the selection of systems methodologies (Chapter 4) and related project management processes (Chapter 5).

Furthermore, our experience has been that even the most detailed and rigorous project management systems will not work effectively unless the relationships between the various people systems and the two control systems (project and management) first are considered and resolved by project people and unless communication channels are designed to facilitate the project control processes that are undertaken by users, management, and teams. Therefore, we now turn our focus to the most important element in project management: people.

TEAM EXERCISE

Crazy Squares

This exercise simulates three typical project team structures, as listed below. It provides an opportunity to consider the relationship between control and communication and the idea that control and information are related.

Note: The first two team structures place restrictions on communication. Consider whether this affects the quality of control existing in each team.

○   Form teams of four to five members into three common structures:

1.   Chief programmer/technical leader structure: B, C, D, and E can communicate only to A.

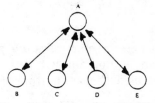

2.   Hierarchical structure: D can communicate only to B. B can communicate to D or A, and so on.

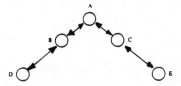

3.   Adaptive structure: Everyone can communicate with one another.

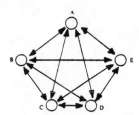

○ Distribute to each team randomly sorted pieces of the five squares shown below.

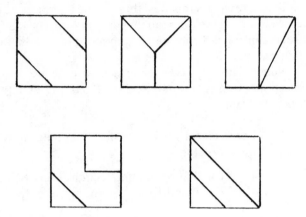

○ Each team must construct five complete squares. A team is not finished until each team member has a completed square in front of him or her.

○ Members may not communicate verbally and can communicate *only* by giving away pieces to another team member.

References: Chapter 2

1. F.P. Brooks, Jr., *The Mythical Man-Month* (Reading, Mass.: Addison-Wesley, 1975), pp. 21-26.

2. W.R. Ashby, *Introduction to Cybernetics* (New York: John Wiley & Sons, 1961).

3. G.M. and D. Weinberg, *On the Design of Stable Systems* (New York: John Wiley & Sons, 1980), p. 329.

4. S. Beer, *Designing Freedom* (New York: John Wiley & Sons, 1974), p. 83.

5. C.E. Shannon and W. Weaver, *The Mathematical Theory of Communication* (Urbana, Ill.: University of Illinois Press, 1949).

6. B.W. Boehm, "Software Engineering — As It Is," *Proceedings of the Fourth International Conference on Software Engineering* (New York: Institute of Electrical and Electronics Engineers, 1979), pp. 11-21.

7. B.P. Lientz and E.B. Swanson, *Software Maintenance Management* (Reading, Mass.: Addison-Wesley, 1980).

8. C.E. Walston and C.P. Felix, "A Method of Programming Measurement and Estimation," *IBM Systems Journal,* Vol. 16, No. 1 (January 1977), pp. 54-73.

9. R. Canning, ed., "What Information Do Managers Need?" *EDP Analyzer,* Vol. 17, No. 6 (June 1979).

10. J.F. Rockart, "Chief Executives Define Their Own Data Needs," *Harvard Business Review,* Vol. 57, No. 2 (March-April 1979), pp. 81-93.

3
People

The team members don't hit one another over the head.

3
People

"Man, not materials, forms the decisive factor."
— **Mao Tse-Tung***

Models of human behavior can be thought of as pairs of glasses that can be used for viewing the world — making sense of it and providing a basis for action. However, there are two problems with choosing glasses: making sure that we have selected the right pair, and making sure that, over time, the glasses still help us see properly. This chapter is about the many pairs of glasses that fit us and fit the people who have taught us. Because this chapter examines human motivation and behavior, it will read at times like a research text on psychology. However, we're not professional psychologists. We're merely people who have shaped our jobs to give us time to read, discuss, observe, and learn — from books and journals, of course, but most importantly from people. We believe that there are powerful insights, *not answers,* to be gained from these models or glasses.[†]

■ Problems with productivity

In our recent project management seminars, we asked some two hundred experienced users, managers, analysts, and programmers to give us their reasons why team members don't work well either as individuals or team members. In brain-storming sessions that followed the seminars, these people provided answers drawn from their own experiences. A consistent set of about seventy reasons emerged from each of the seminar groups, regardless of job category. These reasons ranged from the practical — lack of skills, lack of machine time, ambiguous specifications — through the managerial — poor job direction, inadequate communication, insufficient people resources, too many interrup-

---

*Lecture, 1938, published in *The Nation,* April 16, 1955.
[†]If none of them fit you, throw them out, and let us know what does fit you!

tions — to the emotional — feeling burnt out, dislike of boss or peers, fear of failure, day-dreaming.

During discussions about the significance of these reasons, four crucial observations emerged:

- At any one point in the project, any number of the seventy-plus reasons will be operating on the project team, reducing the team's productivity and morale.

- Many of these reasons can have either positive or negative impacts on different team members depending on the team members' perspectives. For example, one team member may not be working well because he feels too challenged and consequently overwhelmed by a task, while another member of the same team may be feeling under-utilized and bored. The project leader may see the reaction of only the first member and so may reduce the number of tasks to be done — a decision that, of course, will make the second member even more unhappy.

Fig. 3.1. The project leader's dilemma.

- If we accept the prevailing view that the project leader is responsible for the team's output, motivation, and control, then we can only conclude that the project leader's task is virtually impossible. First, he or she has to handle the interrelationships between team members (with five team members, ten relationships are possible*). Second, the leader has to be aware of the complex implications of the potential impact on work conditions by the positive and negative factors described above. Third, it is extremely difficult for the leader to solve or even minimize the cause of many of the reasons cited.

- Most important of all, the project leader has to handle the impact of the seventy-plus reasons on himself or herself — a point illustrated in the following extract from a diary kept by an extremely competent project leader in an organization we visited recently: "Productivity was low this week. I caught a bad cold, I fell off my bicycle, and I fell in love!" She admitted that she wasn't particularly concerned about project productivity during that week. Who could blame her?

Beer once commented that traditional hierarchical structures make people's heads get bigger as they move upward in the organization [1]. We believe from our experience with hundreds of project workers that traditional structures can also require people to become *less human* as they gain responsibility and higher positions in their organizations.†

The situation is obviously not as bleak as we have shown it. Project teams do, in fact, work together to produce systems; but it is essential to realize that because of the reasons mentioned earlier in the chapter, project teams in general are not realizing their full human or work potential. Interestingly, problems are handled within project teams often just by people listening to one another's problems; we believe that, in most cases, it's the *team,* and not the leader, that recognizes and attends to many of its problems. We believe, furthermore, that the reason for this is that teams are composed of people who care for their coworkers, and *who don't switch off as human beings when they get to work.*

Again, we come back to our belief that it is people, *not* project control systems, who plan, develop, maintain, and manage systems. These systems that project workers develop are for other people to use. People! People! People! Project management is about people using

---

*Based on the number of one-to-one communications, the number of relationships between n people is $n(n-1) \div 2$.
†This is a variation on the Peter Principle [2], which states that people advance to one level above their level of competence or, applied to data processing, the best programmers become the worst managers.

systems, and it is about what motivates them, as well as about what discourages them.

Fig. 3.2. Project leaders are not meant to be people.

■ **Behavior, values, and needs**

Since the early 1940s, some very important insights into the psychological behavior of individuals, as well as their interactions with others, have emerged. These insights have often conflicted, and contemporary psychology and sociology appear to have split into opposing factions: behaviorist versus humanist, individual versus organization, and so on.* What we have found from working with teams is that from these often conflicting factions, some common ideas can be distilled.

Figure 3.3 gives a valuable overview of the complex of interacting factors that influence human behavior. What this model demonstrates is simply that when a person reacts to a situation, it is never because of one isolated factor. Perception of the real situation is filtered by the individual's feeling, seeing, and thinking; reactions are determined ultimately according to each person's value system. Value systems, therefore, are crucial to the whole environment of project control, as they provide the basis for each person's actions and beliefs. To effect changes in value systems requires changes in the way each person feels, sees, and thinks.

---

*This is typical of systems survival behavior described in Chapter 1 as "what is the whole is a function of who's looking at it."

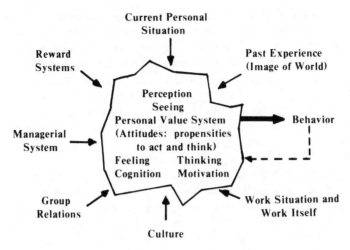

Fig. 3.3. Factors influencing behavior.

Many studies of value systems have been undertaken, and there is growing evidence of the existence of two sets of value systems or paradigms. Table 3.1, based on the work of Trist [3] and Argyris and Schon [4], shows the significant differences between the two paradigms.

Table 3.1
Two Prevailing Organizational Paradigms

OLD PARADIGM	NEW PARADIGM
The technological imperative	Joint optimization
People as an extension of the machine	The machine as an extension of people
People seen as interchangeable spare parts	People seen as an asset to be developed
Maximum task breakdown, division of narrow and single skills	Optimum task grouping; inter-disciplinary teams; multiple, broad skills
External controls (super-visors, specialist staffs, procedures)	Internal controls (self-regulating subsystems)
Tall organization chart, autocratic style	Flat organization chart, participative style
Competition, gamesmanship	Collaboration, congeniality
Information hidden for use as power	Information shared to facilitate cooperation
Alienation	Commitment
Low risk-taking	Innovation

Researchers* have shown that the organizational and power structures of project teams, organizations, and societies reflect adherence to one or the other of the two models in the table. For example, bureaucratic/hierarchical structures reflect the old paradigm (competitive) values. We need not concentrate in this book on the well-known and serious failings of bureaucratic/hierarchical systems; it is our belief that we live with their dehumanizing and inefficient results each day. By contrast, there is no question in our minds that systems developed using new paradigm behaviors, as shown in Table 3.1, are more efficient, responsive, creative, fun, and human.†

Within the broad perspective of value systems, we now need to consider the relationship between individual motivation, performance, job satisfaction, leadership roles, and team structures. The work of Maslow [7] and Lewin [11] in the late 1940s is central to this examination; they produced basic models of human needs and group behavior, drawn from their questioning of what makes people grow and work in a creative, human manner.‡ Maslow suggested the existence of five basic needs, and asserted that people are motivated by a desire to fulfill these needs in a *healthy* way. These five needs relate to psychological growth; and as one need is satisfied to an acceptable extent, another need becomes of primary importance. The satisfactory achievement of successively higher needs requires psychological growth.

The first need is *physiological* (to survive as an organism), with the second being *security* for this physiological need and a fixed framework for its continued satisfaction. The third need to emerge is that of social belonging and *acceptance/love* from other people — be it family, lover, friends, or work group. Once an individual has been accepted within a group, that individual's need for *esteem*, the need to be valued within that group or relationship, appears to become predominant. With this need fulfilled, the final and strongest motivating psychological need emerges: the need for *self-actualization* (the need to be one's own self). While there appears to be a consensus on the basic validity of Maslow's model of needs, contemporary research has grouped individual motivational needs into two broad categories: extrinsic and intrinsic. The diagram in Fig. 3.4 shows the relationships of the basic needs.

---

*Of particular note is the research of Argyris and Schon [4], McGregor [5], Rogers [6], and Maslow [7].
†Refer to Rogers [6], Weinberg [8], Greenbaum [9], and Harman [10].
‡Maslow's work formed the foundation for subsequent studies by Herzberg [12], McGregor [5], Vroom [13], and Cherns [14]. Indeed, Maslow's work on motivation and Lewin's on democratic groups have provided the basis for most recent work in organizational and individual behavior.

The present structure of our society is such that work is the primary source for satisfying these needs. We know from our research that most programming jobs today can satisfy at least the support needs, as well as a significant portion of the social needs, of people.* Indeed, many project members with whom we have spoken value the people they work with (with, not for) above *all* other variables in their jobs. In other words, most project workers have satisfied their extrinsic needs to an acceptable level, and thus the relationship between project performance, job satisfaction, and intrinsic needs becomes the essential consideration for project management.

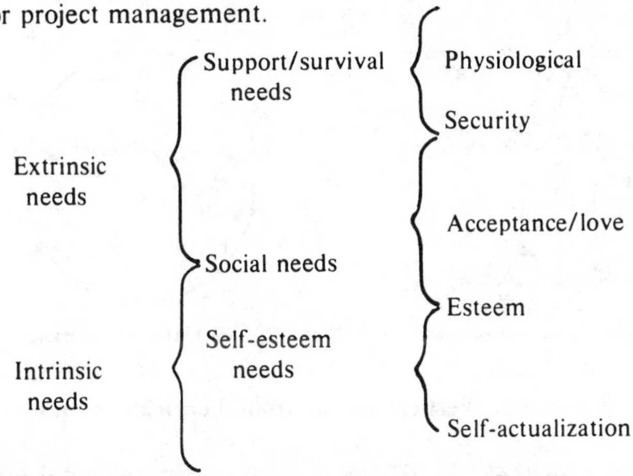

Extrinsic needs
Support/survival needs — Physiological, Security

Social needs — Acceptance/love, Esteem

Intrinsic needs
Self-esteem needs — Self-actualization

Fig. 3.4. Contemporary view of motivational needs.

■ **Satisfaction and project performance**

Earlier attempts at improving job performance and satisfaction concentrated on the vertical and/or horizontal enrichment of jobs [14, 16, 17]. Horizontal enrichment involved grouping tasks that were previously performed by individuals and forming a team to share responsibility for all tasks. Thus, in Fig. 3.5, for example, member C could share any of the tasks done by the team, rather than perform task Y alone. Vertical enrichment involved incorporating all or some of the traditional tasks performed by project leaders, for example, planning, scheduling, and assigning tasks, into the team's area of responsibility. In most cases of vertical enrichment within organizations, the tradition-

---

*This observation should be qualified: With the continuing introduction of improved employee working conditions and increased benefits, as well as with modern-day technological advances, this becomes less true. Today, quality-of-working-life issues contribute in increasingly greater amounts to the overall satisfaction of human needs.

al supervisory functions were devolved to the team, leaving the "boundary rider" functions, those functions pertaining to inter-team communication and coordination and senior management relations, for management to absorb. The shift to a project team approach in many computing shops was an intuitive horizontal, and occasionally vertical, job enrichment process.

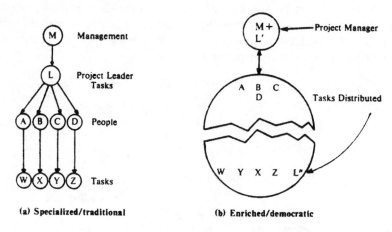

Fig. 3.5. Vertical and horizontal enrichment of jobs.

Although these horizontal and vertical enrichment attempts have been demonstrated to lead to greater job satisfaction, other research [18] has found that improved job satisfaction does not necessarily lead to improved performance. It is becoming evident from our own observations and from research [9, 14, 17] that the combination of satisfied extrinsic needs (improved pay scales, working conditions, and social interaction) coupled with the lack of responsibility, autonomy, and feedback typical of most bureaucratic organizations, together with a general change in society's attitudes toward the importance of having leisure time, has *forced* many previously dedicated project people to adopt a limited commitment to their work. As an experienced project leader said during one of our seminars, "My job pays the bills and leaves me free to do what I really want to do outside work."

Vroom suggested that if the satisfaction of needs is related to job performance, then productivity can be improved by recognition of needs followed by supportive action [13]. For example, if a project team believes that its prime function is to build systems that work on time for users (an intrinsic need), then giving it the opportunity and support necessary to do so will significantly enhance that team's level of performance and degree of satisfaction. From our work with hundreds of teams, we believe that the inability of most organizations to let a team do its job properly, — that is, to endow a team with adequate responsibility, resources, tools, and realistic deadlines — is the single most de-motivating influence in the computing profession. If you have never had the opportunity to complete a project properly and to see the smiles on your team members' and users' faces, then fishing, growing roses, or being secretary of the Guild of Tiddly-Winks Makers becomes a very attractive alternative indeed for the satisfaction of higher-level needs. *We don't blame you if you choose the attractive alternative!* We also don't blame you if you don't want to take on leadership responsibility, for doing so might move you further from the work you may be most qualified and happy in doing — to be compensated only by comparatively marginal returns in money or status.

Yet, significant insights have been reported recently regarding the design of organizations and jobs, identifying five essential elements, called core job dimensions, that lead to increased efficiency, higher levels of performance, and increased satisfaction with work.* The characteristics are

- skill variety: an optimal number of different tasks that permit interest and challenge, and at the same time enable the establishing of a work rhythm

- task identity: perceivable and understandable tasks that are performable

- task significance: tasks that are useful and meaningful and that cannot be done by a robot or trained monkey

- autonomy: adequate freedom to take responsibility for and make decisions on what, when, and how tasks are to be done

- feedback: feeling of mutual respect and support from people at all levels in a collaborative, rather than competitive, environment

These five elements work together symbiotically to produce an environment conducive to learning and growth, an environment that facilitates learning from the nature of the five criteria above and that fosters a

---

*These core job dimensions were developed by Hackman and Oldham [19]. They have been used successfully by Mumford [20], Emery [17], and Hackman, et al. [21] to evaluate the satisfaction-level of jobs and to redesign jobs, and recently by Couger and Zawacki [22] to evaluate programmer attitudes.

desire for growth. (Significantly, project work inherently has all of the necessary elements.)

These criteria are incorporated into the socio-technical systems design approach developed by Mumford [16] and Taylor [23]; the result is an integrated model of project team design, as shown in Fig. 3.6.*

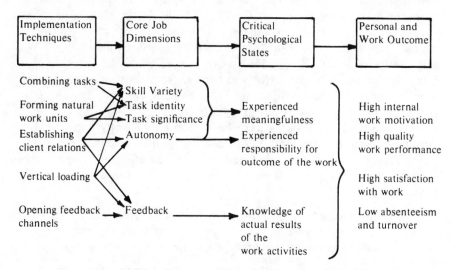

Fig. 3.6. An integrated model including implementation techniques.

We will explore the implementation of this integrated model in Chapters 6 and 7. However, we can use it now to consider team structures and leadership roles.

■ Roles in a project team

In Weinberg's seminal book, *The Psychology of Computer Programming* [8], he introduced the concept of the adaptive team to the computing profession. This concept includes all of the elements of the model detailed in Fig. 3.6, and has as its fundamental requirement that ". . . the determinants of leadership are based on the inner realities of team life, not imposed from the outside."† Our experience is that the most difficult feature of adaptive teams and the most serious objection to the concept that is raised by programmers and management is the *concern for leadership roles.*

---

*This model is based on work not only by Mumford and Taylor, but also by Hackman, et al. [21].
†G.M. Weinberg, op. cit., p. 81.

At the beginning of this chapter, we examined how hierarchical (and chief programmer) team structures force many people into extremely difficult and dehumanizing leadership positions. The common myth is that adaptive teams imply anarchic rabbles with no person designated as the "responsible" leader. Constantine and Constantine [24], in a study of successful communal groups, suggest that in order for a group, a team, a family, or an organization to survive, a set of *leadership functions,* or roles, has to exist, identified and defined as follows:

- chairperson/moderator: calls and adjourns meetings, keeps things to the point, comments on points of order, recognizes people who want to speak, and so on

- spokesperson/liaison/gatekeeper: corresponds on behalf of the group, initiates and mediates with outside contacts, handles public opinion, and represents team opinion

- organizer/manager: takes charge when things need to be done, sets up and maintains schedules, and handles process-oriented crises

- group maintenance person/"den mother": provides the social binding for the group, recognizes people for what they are, rather than what they do; provides a shoulder to cry on; channels non-work information

- technical leader/theoretician: resolves technical issues, provides a source for learning and a last resort in disputes, and formulates broad design philosophies

- entrepreneur/planner: looks for areas of possible improvement and for long-term implications of changes in environment, considers alternative futures, and designs and evaluates new techniques

Similar, perhaps less radical, sets of leadership roles have been developed by Mintzberg [25] and by Keen and Morton [26]. Both views highlight the diversity of leadership roles, and more significantly, both point out an interesting problem in psychology: If we assume, as seems to be the situation in many organizations, that one person is responsible and rewarded for performing these roles, then the ideal leader would need to be a psychologist/super-programmer with schizophrenic tendencies. Stress-related disorders, nervous and mental breakdowns, and other, more subtle casualty symptoms so prevalent among people in leadership positions indicates that the psychological, physical, and intellectual requirements of leadership are simply beyond many people's capabilities.*

Fig. 3.7. Who wants to be a project leader?

In order for a project team to work well, there must be psychological, administrative, and technical leaders. It is naive and foolish to suggest that one person can perform all these areas equally well. Further, in many computer shops people are promoted to project leader and manager positions not on their ability to manage, but rather on their technical abilities. Some organizations have recognized this problem and are implementing matrix team approaches that provide separate career structures and responsibilities for technical and administrative people.†

The reality is that, in a well-functioning team, these areas of responsibility are shared and, in general, the required leadership role is performed by the person best suited to the roles required at that time *regardless of status in the formal organization.* The roles of technical leader and of organizer/manager may continue to be seen as the significant ones. However, by recognizing the equal importance of *all*

---

*Selye's work on stress [27] is particularly interesting. Selye uses many of the systems approaches discussed in Chapter 1 of this book. Also, Forbes [28] concentrates on executive work and stress problems. The difficulties of leadership are not peculiar just to programmers and other project people.
†Daly [29] outlines the implementation of a matrix project team structure.

of the roles and by letting technical people lead when the problem is technical and people-oriented members lead when the problem is people, the majority of team members with whom we have worked find Weinberg's concept of shifting leadership more efficient, more humane, and more sensible than traditional project leader structures.

> *The third step in successful project management is to let teams evolve to form their natural structure, within which technical leaders do technical leading, administrators do administration, communicators communicate, and social people do social things. In addition, organizations must give such teams sufficient time and resources for learning, growing, getting on with the job, and enjoying it.*

Having made the investment of time and resources in the team's development, organizations then must begin to safeguard this highly creative and efficient asset, for example, by rewarding the team with the most powerful of all rewards — a more challenging project — rather than disbanding the team prior to or upon completion of the project.

TEAM EXERCISE

Pins and Straws

We have assigned the following exercise to hundreds of people who have found it to be a particularly powerful and enjoyable simulation. It is designed to explore the impact of leadership styles on product quality and team morale.

Some words of caution: It is very difficult for most people to adopt the autocratic style. Also, the "don't care" style involves neither helping or hindering the team; it's a passive role.

- O Form three teams of three to six members and let each select a leader.

- O Ask these leaders to adopt a particular leadership style, for example, democratic, autocratic, and "don't care."

- O Using drinking straws and straight pins, the groups must construct an "edifice" that is to be judged on height, strength, and beauty. Allow ten minutes for construction.

- O After completing the building, each team member must rate leadership style, personal satisfaction with the product, and his or her own level of involvement in the construction.

- O Spend some time discussing the relationship between each leader's style, product quality, and how the teams felt about the exercise.

References: Chapter 3

1. S. Beer, *Designing Freedom* (New York: John Wiley & Sons, 1974), p. 73.

2. L.J. Peter and R. Hull, *The Peter Principle: Why Things Go Wrong* (New York: William Morrow & Co., 1969).

3. E.L. Trist, unpublished paper presented at the Sixth International Personnel Conference, Montreal, November 1977.

4. C. Argyris and D.A. Schon, *Theory in Practice: Increasing Professional Effectiveness* (San Francisco: Jossey Bass, 1974).

5. D. McGregor, *The Human Side of Enterprise* (New York: McGraw-Hill, 1960).

6. C. Rogers, *Carl Rogers on Personal Power* (New York: Delacorte Press, 1977).

7. A. Maslow, *The Farther Reaches of Human Nature* (New York: Penguin Books, 1971).

8. G.M. Weinberg, *The Psychology of Computer Programming* (New York: Van Nostrand Reinhold, 1971).

9. J.M. Greenbaum, *In the Name of Efficiency: Management Theory and Shopfloor Practice in Data-Processing Work* (Philadelphia: Temple University Press, 1979).

10. W. Harman, "The Nature of Our Changing Society," *Management of Change and Conflict*, J.M. Thomas and W. Bennis, eds. (Harmondsworth, Middlesex, England: Penguin Books, 1972), pp. 43-91.

11. K. Lewin, "Frontiers in Group Dynamics," *Human Relations*, Vol. 1, No. 1 (1947), pp. 5-41.

12. F. Herzberg, *The Managerial Choice: To Be Efficient and to Be Human* (Homewood, Ill.: Dow Jones-Irwin, 1976).

13. V.H. Vroom, "The Nature of the Relationship Between Motivation and Performance," *Management and Motivation*, V.H. Vroom and E.L. Deci, eds. (New York: Penguin Books, 1972), pp. 229-36.

14. A. Cherns, "The Principles of Socio-technical Design," *Human Relations*, Vol. 29, No. 8 (1976), pp. 783-92.

15. J.R. Hackman and E.E. Lawler, "Job Change and Motivation: A Conceptual Framework," *Design of Jobs,* L.E. Davis and J.C. Taylor, eds. (New York: Penguin Books, 1972), pp. 75-84.

16. E. Mumford, "A Strategy for the Redesign of Work," *Personnel Review,* Vol. 5, No. 2 (Spring 1976), pp. 33-39.

17. F.E. and M. Emery, *Participative Design — Work and Community Life* (Canberra: Centre for Continuing Education, 1975).

18. L. Porter and E.E. Lawler, "Antecedent Attitudes of Effective Management Performance," *Management and Motivation,* V.H. Vroom and E.L. Deci, eds. (New York: Penguin Books, 1972), pp. 253-64.

19. J.R. Hackman and G. Oldham, "Development of the Job Diagnostic Survey," *Journal of Applied Psychology,* Vol. 60 (1975), pp. 159-70.

20. E. Mumford, "Computer Systems and Work Design: Problems of Philosophy and Vision," *Personnel Review,* Vol. 3, No. 2 (Spring 1974), pp. 40-49.

21. J.R. Hackman, G. Oldham, R. Janson, and K. Purdy, "A New Strategy for Job Enrichment," *California Management Review,* Vol. 17, No. 4 (1975), pp. 57-71.

22. J.D. Couger and R.A. Zawacki, "What Motivates DP Professionals?" *Datamation,* Vol. 24, No. 9 (September 1978), pp. 116-23.

23. J. Taylor, "The Human Side of Work: The Socio-Technical Approach to Work System Design," *Personnel Review,* Vol. 4, No. 3 (Summer 1975), pp. 17-22.

24. L.L. and J.M. Constantine, *Group Marriage* (New York: Macmillan, 1973).

25. H. Mintzberg, *The Nature of Managerial Work* (New York: Harper & Row, 1973).

26. P.G.W. Keen and M.S.S. Morton, *Decision Support Systems: An Organizational Perspective* (Reading, Mass.: Addison-Wesley, 1978).

27. H. Selye, *The Stress of Life* (New York: McGraw-Hill, 1956).

28. R. Forbes, *Corporate Stress: How to Manage Stress and Make It Work for You* (New York: Doubleday, 1979).

29. E.B. Daly, "Organizing for Successful Software Development," *Datamation,* Vol. 25, No. 14 (December 1979), pp. 106-20.

4
Systems
Methodologies

The team members report on progress.

4
Systems
Methodologies

"Better one safe way than a hundred on which you cannot reckon." — **Aesop***

Weinberg observed that the data processing industry in the early Seventies ". . . saw the gradual movement of programming from private works of art to corporate assets."[†] Accordingly, the emergence of new techniques such as structured analysis, design, and coding, coupled with an increasing demand for accountability and product review techniques, shifted the emphasis in computing toward more predictable engineering-like concepts. Increasingly, the tools and techniques of computer systems development are being integrated into consistent and rigorous methodologies that not only provide assistance to project teams in doing the work but also provide a base for managing the project.

■ Life stages of a system

To begin our discussion of systems development methodologies, we first need to consider the total "life" of a system, which has the general structure illustrated in Fig. 4.1. The development stage encompasses the analysis, design, and implementation of a system. Development is followed by the enhancement stage — a euphemistic name for that period during which occurs the incorporation of overlooked or inadequately specified systems functions and the debugging and tuning of the installed system. The final stage is called the degradation stage, the period during which adaptive and upgrade maintenance is typically performed. This stage, which we believe consumes much of the typical

---

*Aesop, "The Fox and the Cat," *The Fables of Aesop*, J. Jacobs, ed. (London: Macmillan, 1979), p. 92.
[†]G.M. Weinberg, "Programming as a Social Activity," unpublished seminar notes, Canberra, 1974.

maintenance effort, attempts to keep the system viable within a changing environment [1, 2].* The degradation stage incorporates clerical support, as well as computer system changes that reflect new demands arising from changes in legislation, for example, or from taxation, financial policies, or equipment and software upgrading.

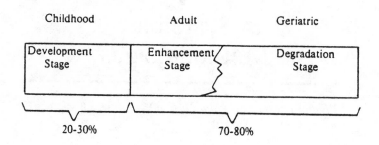

Fig. 4.1. Passages: the life stages of systems.

In this chapter, we examine only the development stage. The latter two stages can be controlled in the same fashion as new projects, with requests for system changes constituting the system specification and with the use of release versions of maintained systems similar to new releases of operating systems and packages.†

Before we look at some modern development techniques, let's look at the history of these techniques.

- **Classic phased approach**

The phased approach to systems development has been used with varying degrees of success since the mid-Sixties. The basic concept of this approach is that the system's life-cycle is broken into perceivable phases, which have defined end conditions or exit criteria. As illustrated in Fig. 4.2 on the next page, the phases consist of separate components connected by feedback loops. A major "go, no-go" decision by management occurs between the feasibility and analysis phases. Our experience is that this approach doesn't work for two major reasons: First, the classic model does not reflect the reality of programming

---

*Recent studies by Boehm [1] in particular have shown that stages 2 and 3 consume fifty to sixty percent of the total data processing effort.
†Lientz and Swanson [3] provides an excellent introduction to the management of stages 2 and 3, and contains comprehensive statistics as supportive evidence.

work. Evidence provided by Boehm [1] and our own experience shows that phases 1 and 2 are either not done in most systems development efforts or at best take ten to twenty percent of the effort. In most cases, phase 1 (the feasibility study) *is totally ignored.* Thirty to forty percent of the effort is devoted to phases 3, 4, and 5, with phases 6, 7, and 8 taking the remaining fifty to sixty percent. Because of a lack of adequate systems analysis and design tools, breakdowns in communications with users, or management pressure to produce something tangible,* programmers move as quickly as possible into the detailed design and coding phases. (This situation was stated precisely by one battle-worn programmer: "The coding's almost finished. We're just about to start on the design.") Further, there is considerable overlap and iteration between the detailed design, coding, and test phases, which result in difficulties in determining when a phase is complete.

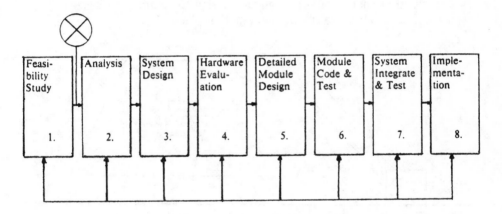

Fig. 4.2. The classic phased model.

The other major reasons for the failure of the classic phased approach are lack of management commitment and lack of understanding of the process of computer systems development, which is unfamiliar to them. Nolan, in his stage hypothesis for computer systems [4], suggests that initial successes with the computerization of simple operational systems, such as payroll or inventory systems, lead to management's unquestioning reliance on data processing professionals, leaving them unsupervised and uncontrolled to practice their "dark art."

---

*In one seminar on structured design in Melbourne in 1976, Larry Constantine referred to this management ploy as WISCA, or Why Isn't Sally Coding Anything?

■ Second-generation phased approach

An unstable period, marked in most organizations by major project disasters, characterized use of the classic phased approach and gave rise to the subsequent development of new programming and systems design methods. The classic phased approach was re-evaluated, and from it a second-generation phased approach evolved. This is best illustrated by the IBM model developed by Metzger [5] and shown in Fig. 4.3. This model for project development includes the following five improvements over the classic model: It accepts the existence of a negotiation phase (between users and programmers), which can consume considerable project resources; it maps some estimation of resource consumption at various stages; it recognizes the iterative nature of the design-code-test implementation process; it emphasizes project planning and control; and it shows the most important checkpoint — the decision at the end of analysis and preliminary design to commit the biggest proportion of resources to the implementation phase.

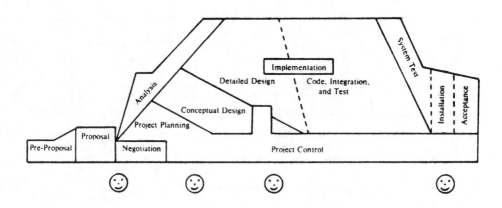

Fig. 4.3. Second-generation phased model.

Major milestones or review points in the systems development process are indicated in Fig. 4.3 by smiling faces. These review points (or "smilestones," as one project team called them) are used by management to check progress to-date and the meeting of objectives, and to re-evaluate estimates and schedules. We suggest that this model is most appropriate for programming shops not using the structured systems development techniques.

The second-generation model refined the concept that the control of projects involves a formal framework or map of perceivable, clearly defined processes, the completion of which can be used to record progress at various levels of abstraction. At the highest level of abstraction is the system or project. The next level is a phase or major process, with the lowest level usually termed a deliverable (see Fig. 4.4), which is a small, precisely defined, quantifiable activity that can be allocated two states: completed (reviewed and working), or not completed.

The concept of deliverables avoids the standard syndrome of a system's being "ninety percent complete" for a long time, and provides inch-pebbles, which can be accumulated to form milestones. A phase is complete when all its deliverables are complete. Examples of deliverables include module design, test-plans, logic specification, analysis models, or reviewed code.

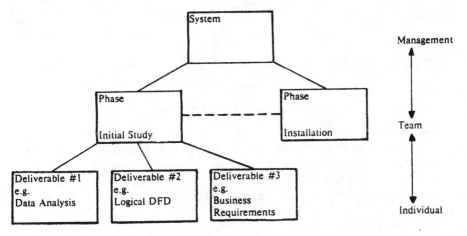

Fig. 4.4. Review and deliverable chart: levels of abstraction.

■ **Third-generation: The emergence of structured methodologies**

The introduction in the mid-Seventies of the structured analysis, data analysis, and top-down versioned implementation approaches was significant in the evolution of systems development methodologies. Additional methodologies, such as business data modeling (termed "information modeling" or "information engineering"*) have resulted in a third-generation model of systems development (see Fig. 4.5, on the following page). Continuing advances in information and enterprise modeling will eventually require a new group of deliverables paralleling structured process analysis deliverables. (We hesitate to say it, but a fourth-generation model is coming.)

---

*Refer to Finkelstein's information engineering approach [6] and Flavin's information modeling approach [7], which both examine business or enterprise requirements as being distinct from specific business functions.

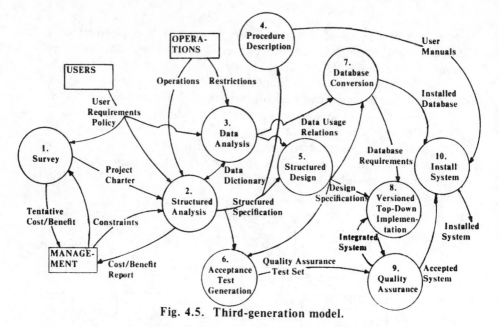

Fig. 4.5. Third-generation model.

The significant difference between the third-generation model and the first- and second-generation approaches is the emphasis on analysis, database modeling, and quality and audit assurance, together with the packaging of these systems development techniques into third-party or vendor-supplied project management packages.

□   *The importance of analysis*

Analysis has been the "poor relation" of computing since its beginning. Studies by Boehm [1] and writings by Canning [8] support our experience that traditional analysis techniques, which are heavily oriented toward machine-solution, often provide vast quantities of reports that are ambiguous and difficult to read. Consequently, they hamper the communication between users and analysts.

Further, Boehm's studies show that errors detected when the system is implemented, rather than when it is only in the analysis stage, cost one hundred times more to correct.* The use of graphic tools such as data-flow diagrams to model the flow of data through processes, of specification techniques for showing the logic of the processes, of project and data dictionaries, of data analysis and accessing techniques, of rigorous design heuristics and review processes — all associated with the new structured analysis-information engineering techniques — pro-

---

*We like the analogy of the relative cost of adding a new bathroom including new plumbing to a completed house compared with adding the bathroom at the blueprint stage.

vide teams with more precisely defined deliverables.* In addition, they enable the business activities under consideration to be modeled in a simple manner that facilitates the communication between users and computer people and the detailing of alternative solutions for evaluation and selection in a cooperative manner.

☐ *A word on packages*

Another important refinement in the area of systems development was the emergence in the late 1970s of a number of third-party systems development methodologies. These packages not only provide a standardized approach to deliverables, which details what and when deliverables are required *and* how to produce them, but also often include standards for coding, review, and documentation, as well as associated project management guidelines (see Chapter 5).

☐ *The concept of versions*

The third-generation stage model also includes the concept of versions suggested by David in 1968.

> "... experience ... has led some people to have the opinion that any software systems that cannot be completed by some four to five people within a year can never be completed; that is, reach a satisfactory steady-state."†

As shown in Fig. 4.6 on the next page, the versioned approach avoids the problem of users, management, and the team's having to wait years for a final working system because it provides interim working systems. Version 1, which may perform input procedures to generate data files with a simulated output process, can be totally implemented. And, while the team is developing version 2, the users can be testing and even using version 1, accessing the data files with software or operating systems packages, for example, and with clerical support systems. The Australian Bureau of Statistics used this approach to develop a large database system for industry statistics, releasing it in three versions. Version 1 handled input and some processing. Version 2 added output and more processing with limited data access capability. The final ver-

---

*DeMarco's *Structured Analysis and System Specification* [9] and Gane and Sarson's *Structured Systems Analysis* [10] provide comprehensive introductions to these techniques.
†E.E. David, Jr., "Design Criteria: Some Thoughts About Production of Large Software Systems," *Software Engineering: Report on a 1968 Conference in Garmisch*, P. Naur and B. Randell, eds. (Brussels, Belgium: NATO Science Committee, 1969), p. 39.

sion added the database facilities. Each release took ten to twelve months to complete. The versioned approach provides the interim proof necessary to assure management, users, and the team itself that they are on the right track. A word of caution, however, is offered: This approach is really viable only if a complete systems model has been developed to enable correct selection of versions [11, 12, 13].

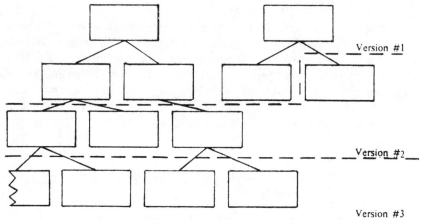

Fig. 4.6. Versioned implementation.*

Citing management's need for visible proof of progress, Kolence commented:

> "The main interest of management is knowing what progress has been made towards reaching the final goal of the project. The difficulty is to identify observable events which mark this progress."[†]

■ Summary

Evidently, projects developed using second- and, in particular, third-generation models and tools are easier to decompose into deliverables, which are observable events, than was possible using the classical approach. With the use of technical reviews and structured walkthroughs[‡] as reviewing processes,

---

*From T. DeMarco's *Concise Notes on Software Engineering* (New York: YOURDON Press, 1979), pp. 51-52. Copyright © 1979 by YOURDON inc. Reprinted by permission.

[†]K. Kolence, "Production Control" conference participant, *Software Engineering*, op. cit., P. Naur and B. Randell, eds., p. 87.

[‡]Technical reviews and structured walkthroughs, which are discussed in Chapter 5, are peer-group reviews of products of the systems development process.

The implementation of a systems development methodology approach as a framework for project information systems provides the fourth step requisite for successful project management.

□   *Overview of software engineering techniques*

From a systems perspective, the third-generation developments in tools, techniques, and team structures have solved the problem of the complexity of computer project work from two aspects as shown in Fig. 4.7. Using Ashby's Law of Requisite Variety [14] as a guide, it appears that some of these developments help reduce the system's complexity while others provide project teams with greater ability to deal with this complexity (or, in Ashby's terms, this greater variety).

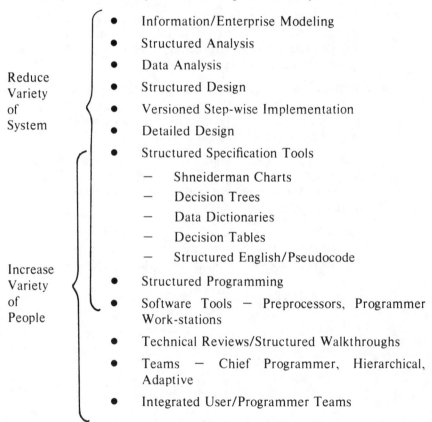

Reduce Variety of System

- Information/Enterprise Modeling
- Structured Analysis
- Data Analysis
- Structured Design
- Versioned Step-wise Implementation
- Detailed Design
- Structured Specification Tools
  - Shneiderman Charts
  - Decision Trees
  - Data Dictionaries
  - Decision Tables
  - Structured English/Pseudocode

Increase Variety of People

- Structured Programming
- Software Tools — Preprocessors, Programmer Work-stations
- Technical Reviews/Structured Walkthroughs
- Teams — Chief Programmer, Hierarchical, Adaptive
- Integrated User/Programmer Teams

Fig. 4.7. Relationship between software engineering and Ashby's Law of Requisite Variety.

TEAM EXERCISE

The Lego® Game

This exercise examines the problems of building systems without a methodology as a framework for construction. It shows the need for a methodology to reflect the reality of the project team's day-to-day activities. To increase realism, managers can play tricks such as taking away members for more crucial projects.

○ Build a model of a man using approximately fifty pieces of red and white Lego blocks, and place it on a central table.

○ Select construction teams of three to six people who can see (but not touch) the model. Ask them to plan the steps and estimate the amount of time needed to reproduce the Lego man.

○ Provide each team with enough building blocks to build a duplicate of the model. When the model is completed, have the team correct errors and add the maintenance time to the team's total time.

○ Assign one person to keep data on the amount of time spent on each of the following activities: planning, analysis, design, implementation, and, of course, maintenance/debugging.

○ Compare the estimates with the actual time, including the time for maintenance, and discuss what the team learned about a methodology for building models.

References: Chapter 4

1. B.W. Boehm, "Software Engineering — As It Is," *Proceedings of the Fourth International Conference on Software Engineering* (New York: Institute of Electrical and Electronics Engineers, 1979), pp. 11-21.

2. B.P. Lientz, E.B. Swanson, and G.E. Tompkins, "Characteristics of Applications Software Maintenance," *Communications of the ACM,* Vol. 21, No. 6 (June 1978), pp. 466-71.

3. B.P. Lientz and E.B. Swanson, *Software Maintenance Management* (Reading, Mass.: Addison-Wesley, 1980).

4. R. Nolan, "Managing the Crises in Data Processing," *Harvard Business Review,* Vol. 57, No. 2 (March-April 1979), pp. 115-26.

5. P. Metzger, *Programming Project Management Guide,* IBM Technical Report No. GA36-0005-1 (Gaithersburg, Md.: July 1974).

6. C. Finkelstein, *Information Systems: The Challenge* (Gordon: Infocom Monograph, 1979).

7. M. Flavin, *Fundamental Concepts of Information Modeling* (New York: YOURDON Press, prepublication draft, 1980).

8. R. Canning, ed., "The Production of Better Software," *EDP Analyzer,* Vol. 17, No. 2 (February 1979).

9. T. DeMarco, *Structured Analysis and System Specification* (New York: YOURDON Press, 1978).

10. C. Gane and T. Sarson, *Structured Systems Analysis: Tools and Techniques* (New York: Improved System Technologies, Inc., 1977).

11. F.T. Baker and H.D. Mills, "Chief Programmer Teams," *Datamation,* Vol. 19, No. 12 (December 1973), pp. 58-61.

12. E. Yourdon, *A Methodology for Software Development* (New York: YOURDON Press, prepublication draft, 1979).

13. T. DeMarco, *Concise Notes on Software Engineering* (New York: YOURDON Press, 1979).

14. W.R. Ashby, *Introduction to Cybernetics* (New York: John Wiley & Sons, 1961).

5
Project
Management Processes

The team members reconstruct the diagram to see the problems.

5
Project
Management Processes

"There are four types of components in any system: believe-able, perceivable, conceivable and leavable." —**Roy Morian***

In this chapter, we begin to integrate control, information, methodologies, and people by considering the processes of project management from the perspective of how they relate to systems methodologies, who undertakes them, and what information the processes use to ensure projects remain in control.

■ Some general observations

The four processes of work definition, planning, tracking, and reporting or reviewing provide information that answers four basic questions: What is to be done? Who is to do it? When must it be done? and, What productivity is expected? If we asked a team to assemble a jigsaw puzzle (as outlined in the team exercise for this chapter), the "what," or first set of information, would be the number and size of the pieces, the objectives that had been set, the types of joints, and the complexity of the picture. The "who," or second set, would reflect team size, experience in jigsaw-puzzle building, and the management environment. The "when" comprises deadlines, allocation of resources, and relationships between building activities. The fourth set, productivity, is really a result of the other three elements.

In our seminars, the jigsaw puzzles we used took seventeen to eighteen minutes to complete for teams of five to eight members, while productivity estimates varied from as few as five to as many as thirty minutes. We noticed that any plans that were made during the planning functions were thrown out and forgotten in the excitement of the

---

*Roy Morian was a student in one of our project seminars.

65

building process and that at least one good jigsaw-puzzle solver either would do the majority of the work or get very bored with the antics of the amateurs on the team and withdraw from the task. Of course, any person attempting to perform management functions was trampled in the rush to complete the puzzle. The second time we played the game, with the same teams, the process was better estimated and better managed, and was accomplished with far fewer difficulties: The teams developed a method of doing jigsaw puzzles; they planned according to it; they reviewed their progress; and they met their objectives.

The points we are making are well known in computing, but they seem to be ignored in many organizations. Therefore, let us briefly re-state these points:

- Estimating is difficult at most times and virtually impossible when the process is unfamiliar to the team members.

- Teams can learn to do tasks better when there is a history of experience readily available to them.

- The actual process of building systems can be so interesting, hurried, or consuming that plans, schedules, and so on often can be forgotten in the rush to complete the project. How many critical projects have you experienced in which there wasn't time to manage or do the job properly?

- The teams can systematize their approach without management having to tell them to do it.

Before we look at the project management processes in more detail, some other general observations are pertinent about their use. First, unless teams write down and store project information, systems development can never begin to be orderly and efficient. This information not only can help in estimating, planning, and similar activities, but it also can be used to combat stupid management decisions. For example, a team was asked to undertake a significant revision to its project — a change that management had promised to users over a congenial lunch. However, this team (unbeknownst to management) had implemented a project-tracking system and was able to show management hard documentation (in the form of computer printout, which helped) to prove that it was already totally committed in resources to the original schedule. Consequently, management was forced to retract its promise to the users and to find an acceptable alternative.

Second, when undertaking the planning and review processes, organizations must learn that people and teams are not mechanical components that can be interchanged like machines with no disruption to the process.* Brooks [2] has shown that degrees of team expertise differ widely; we must recognize that "experience" is a very dangerous concept. As an old saying goes, "Ten years' experience can be just that or one year's experience ten times over."† Organizations need to understand their employees' specific experience‡ and to recognize that a reputation for being a super-programmer in reality may be a reputation for producing huge amounts of unmaintainable code.

■ **Processes of project management**

The four processes of work definition, planning, tracking, and reporting or reviewing must *all* be undertaken for complete project management. In the same manner that systems methodologies provide a framework for teams to develop systems, these processes provide the operating framework for project management. The quality of project management is directly related to the quality of information that these processes generate (and use in the form of feedback):

- The work definition process develops and maintains a standard methodology as well as other standards (for example, for coding, database administration, and general documentation) as a guide for the planning process. This process is also used to collect software metrics, which are measures of productivity and which we discuss later in this chapter, and Walston and Felix software factors [4]. Both software metrics and factors can affect the project's level of difficulty.

- The planning process includes the activities of planning, estimating, and scheduling. To complete these activities, the planning process may involve customizing a standard systems development methodology for the project, accessing the corporate project file for software metrics from previous projects, and, of

---

*In an important study, Sackman, Erikson, and Grant [1] showed that the productivity of some programmers can be as much as twenty-five times that of other programmers.
†We would hasten to add that with the rapid changes in computing, ten years' experience may also mean ten years' obsolescence.
‡The research of Freedman, Gause, and Weinberg [3] is particularly relevant in this regard.

course, channeling as input the systems requirements and management constraints.

- The tracking process involves monitoring actual performance and, in some cases, handling minor schedule and resource-requirement revisions that can be accommodated by the team. This process also provides quality assurance through technical reviews and walkthroughs and is used to maintain the project history file, which provides updated software metrics for the corporate project file.

- The reporting/reviewing process stores, analyzes, and filters information on project progress fed to it by the tracking process. It compares actual with expected performance, and yields relevant information for the suitable regulatory bodies (team, management, users, computer operations, and so on). The reporting/reviewing process provides a coordinated review across all projects. Through it, the project progress is approved at critical points (for example, completion of detailed analysis), and the process reveals when updates of the systems methodology are required.

The relationships of these four processes are depicted in Fig. 5.1. We now can proceed to a more detailed discussion of each process.

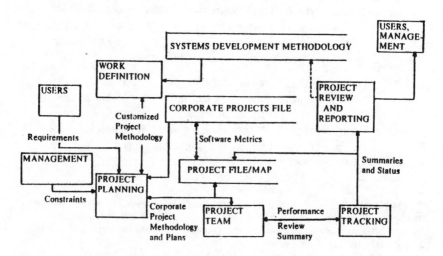

Fig. 5.1. Processes of project management.

☐ *Work definition and planning*

Within the framework provided by the organization's systems methodology, the team members, in conjunction with management and users, must plan, estimate, and schedule the production of a series of deliverables. These deliverables provide the basic building blocks for project work and management. In many cases, a particular project may not require all the deliverables outlined in the systems methodology. For example, smaller projects may not require equipment and software acquisition activities or database modeling. In this case, the planning process not only requires management and user concurrence on schedules and similar matters but also requires agreement on the tailored or customized methodology required for the project. The work definition and planning processes are critical as they provide the framework for the tracking and review processes that follow them.

Depending on organization and management style, the project manager and/or teams produce a project map (to be publicly viewed and reviewed), which shows estimates, deliverable interrelationships and timing dependencies, and the allocation of resources to deliverables. Depending on project size, the project team may use network packages, bar-charts, and similar scheduling tools to assist in deriving the project map.*

Fig. 5.2. The project map.

---

*Network packages provide automated critical path analysis facilities for showing the critical time relations between events (the completion of a deliverable).

It is also important for the project map to be *dynamic:* Through the normal processes of iterative analysis, design, and implementation changes, resource problems, user or environment changes, and estimation errors, the project map will require constant updating and revision. Storable copies of each version of the project map should be kept in the project history file together with the reasons for revision. We have seen such ingenious techniques for storing historical project maps as photographs of white-board bar-charts taken before and after updating.

☐ *Project tracking and review*

We believe project tracking is best achieved through regular team meetings that are recorded by someone acting as secretary. In these meetings, the project map is updated, schedules are amended, and resource allocations are made. The tracking process involves evaluation of expected progress in deliverables against actual progress. The timing of tracking meetings or reports should be tailored to the project. For example, it could be self-defeating to track a six-month deliverable on a three-month cycle. At worst, you could be three months or fifty percent behind before you became aware of any problems. To prevent such problems, the tracking process is used to update the project map and project file, and to report to the review process.

The form and information content of messages to the reporting/reviewing process will reflect the prevailing management style in the project. Two general points are pertinent in this regard: First, top management's information needs, although seeming to be consistent across organizations, may need to be presented using different techniques. Some senior management people prefer "hard" information — forms, reports, and statistics — while others are more comfortable gathering "soft" information from face-to-face meetings and conversations.* Second, regardless of whether management prefers hard or soft information reporting or a combination of both methods, the main information needs of management are straightforward:

- Is the project on schedule?

- If not, can the team handle the schedule slippage within its own area of responsibility, or does management need to do something to help the project return to an in-control state?

---

*See Rockart's work on hard/soft management information reporting [5].

In addition, the review process is required to make major "go, no-go" decisions at the end of each phase or major deliverable.

□   *A word on review information*

In many cases, the teams are forced by badly designed project management systems to pass vast quantities of data (such as the number of hours team members have worked per day or the names and numbers of employees on sick leave) to management, who then must sift through the jumble of figures to isolate the two pieces of information pertaining to schedule and control described above.

a. project information   b. project information
    belongs to management   belongs to team

Fig. 5.3. Who needs to know what?

To illustrate, let's assume that X is the information needed to keep the project in control: X will consist of information on who is doing what and when according to the planned outline in the project map, as well as identification of problem areas, possible solutions, project complexity, and anticipated developments in the next reporting period. Ashby's Law of Requisite Variety, which we introduced in Chapter 2, tells us that we *must* know this information in order to keep the project in control. As shown in Fig. 5.3b, the team should be the main source of this information and should be responsible for its collection and for acting upon it. In fact, we have observed that many successful teams use two information systems: one that the team actually uses to gather X, and one that management believes they, that is, management, need to give them the data in order to find X (if they have the time!).

> *The fifth step in effective project management is the use of the four processes of work definition, planning, tracking, and review by teams to provide project status information to management.*

As we've said before, management's information should be a filtered subset of the information that the team needs; and surprisingly, if you or the team filter the information effectively, management will thank you for reducing the workload, will actually look at the information to make sensible decisions, and will let you know what's happening as a result.

■ Recent developments

We promised at the start to keep this book brief. Rather than detail the developments in the important areas of software metrics, estimation, and reviews, we will summarize the promising breakthroughs in each area.

□ *Software metrics*

Work by Walston and Felix [4], Chrysler [6], Gilb [7], and DeMarco [8] has isolated a series of measurements of data that are significant for software projects. These measurements relate to complexity and productivity levels, and are called software metrics. Some are listed below:

- number of lines of executable code
- work-hours to complete a deliverable*
- staff/team size
- cost limitation
- Walston and Felix factors that include user interface complexity, number of user-originated design changes, personnel experience with application area, and percentage of work subject to walkthroughs.[†]

---

*Work-hours will be different from hours-at-work. Work-hours pertain to time spent actually working on the project, whereas hours-at-work encompass breaks and other non-task related activities. Our evidence is that managers spend ten to thirty percent of the total hours-at-work on projects, with this percentage increasing to a maximum of seventy percent for some team members. This is supported in studies on activities of managers by Mintzberg [9] and Keen and Morton [10].
[†]Walston and Felix list twenty-eight factors in all that have had significant influence on levels of productivity in more than sixty projects. [4].

Since all these metrics can influence the project's development time, they should be considered and evaluated when planning and estimating the systems effort. Figures should be revised, measured, and stored in the project history file throughout the project to enable the development of a set of software metrics for a particular organization.

☐   *Estimation*

There are two significant new concepts in the area of estimation. One is the idea of creeping commitment or multi-stage estimation. The concept is very simple and powerful, and Putnam and Fitzsimmons [11] have provided some excellent ideas on statistical deviation and probability techniques for estimation at three stages (see Fig. 5.4).

Taking into account a series of project variables (see the preceding discussion of software metrics), the team gives three estimates of project time and resources as the project develops.

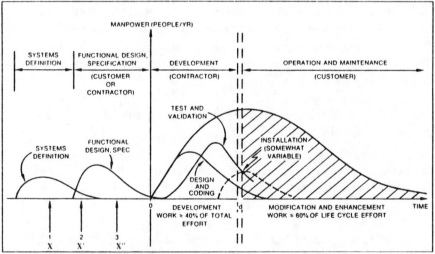

Note: X, X', X'' are author's annotations.

Fig. 5.4. Estimates with decreasing statistical deviation and increasing probability of accuracy.*

As shown in the figure, the first estimate, X, at the beginning of analysis will have a margin of error ± Y (where Y could be anywhere between fifty to one hundred percent of X). The next, X', made at the beginning of broad design, will obviously be more realistic, with Y' being between ten and fifty percent; and the final estimate, X'', made after the completion of design, should be within ten percent (Y'') of the final actual figure. These estimates can be mapped along with probability estimates of accuracy as well.

The second new concept in the area of estimation deals with a set of broad estimating rules, as follows:

- Estimating is different from regurgitating.

- Estimating is different from negotiating.

- Estimations are not subject to bargaining.

- Estimating is different from dividing a fixed duration into component parts.

- A slip in one project phase implies a proportionate slip in all subsequent phases.

- If you want a meaningful answer from someone, don't tell him "the answer."

- A useful planning estimate is a projection that is as likely to be too pessimistic as it is to be too optimistic.

- The ratio between the most optimistic estimate and a useful planning estimate is fairly uniform for any individual.

- Estimate by committee. . . . Throw away the estimate by the person directly responsible for the effort. Average the others.*

These broad rules, coupled with the factors being identified through software metrics and the techniques of Putnam and Fitzsimmons [11], provide a positive step toward clearing up problems with estimating.

□   *Review techniques*

Of all the techniques to emerge in the early 1970s, technical reviews and structured walkthroughs are probably the most useful and successful. They both involve the formal evaluation of *each* deliverable in a system by a small review team, which is made up of people who are familiar with the deliverable and who meet to identify problem areas in the product.

---

*Reprinted by permission. From T. DeMarco's *Structured Analysis and System Specification* (New York: YOURDN Press, 1978), pp. 336-38. Copyright © 1978, 1979 by YOURDN inc.

Technical reviews and walkthroughs evolved from Weinberg's concept of egoless programming [12]. Weinberg observed that people tend to psychologically own their products, thus making it difficult for them to critically evaluate the correctness and readability of their work. Weinberg's idea was that no product was approved until some other person or group had reviewed it.

Technical reviews differ from structured walkthroughs [13] in that the individual producer or team is *not* present; however, both techniques require the review group to have formal roles such as chairperson and scribe, a mix of participant experience, time limitations on the review, and the production of two critical reports: a summary for management and the team on the quality of the product (for example, was it accepted as submitted? was it revised? was it rejected?) and a list of issues and errors for the individual producer or the team.

Research at IBM [14, 15] and observations from our own experience have shown that not only do reviews and walkthroughs reveal errors before systems are implemented, but they also provide essential quality assurance, improve team cohesion, and provide a forum for learning and developing acceptable standards.

It is recommended that technical reviews and walkthroughs be used throughout the system life-cycle (from initial study to maintenance) [16] and as shown in Fig. 5.5, the summary reports can be the primary source for updating the project map during tracking.

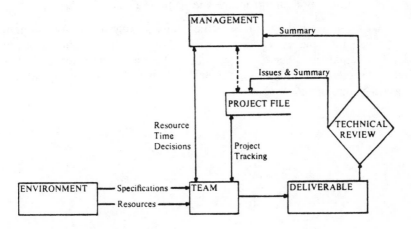

Fig. 5.5. Technical reviews and project tracking.

These techniques are a significant development in project tracking and review, as not only do they indicate that deliverables are completed, but also that they are a quality-assured product.

TEAM EXERCISE

The Jigsaw-Puzzle Game

This exercise models the four processes of project management. The exercise leader can perform the overall review process while the teams and their leaders undertake planning, work definition, and tracking.

○ From each team of six to ten members, select a leader who must estimate how much time his team will need to assemble a jigsaw puzzle as depicted in the completed drawing on the puzzle box. All leaders must have the same puzzle.

○ Each leader, assisted by a librarian or back-up, then must instruct his team, which has been divided into subgroups of two or three, how to build the jigsaw puzzle using randomly allocated pieces.

○ Do not permit the subgroups to see the picture of the completed puzzle or to communicate with members of other subgroups for the first five minutes.

○ After five minutes, the leader can merge the subgroups into any team structure she or he feels is suitable.

To more accurately simulate the real-world systems environment, leaders can hide pieces, change the rules, or alter the deadlines. Compare the actual time needed to complete the puzzle with the estimated times. Discuss a methodology for building, tracking, and reviewing the "jigsaw-puzzle life-cycle."

References: Chapter 5

1. H. Sackman, W.J. Erikson, and E.E. Grant, "Exploratory Experimental Studies Comparing On-line and Off-line Programming Performance," *Communications of the ACM*, Vol. 11, No. 1 (January 1968), pp. 3-11.

2. F.P. Brooks, Jr., *The Mythical Man-Month* (Reading, Mass.: Addison-Wesley, 1975), pp. 21-26.

3. D. Freedman, D. Gause, and G. Weinberg, "Organizing and Training for a New Software Development Project . . . That First Big Step," *Proceedings of the 1977 National Computer Conference*, Vol. 46 (Montvale, N.J.: AFIPS Press, 1977), pp. 255-59.

4. C.E. Walston and C.P. Felix, "A Method of Programming Measurement and Estimation," *IBM Systems Journal*, Vol. 16, No. 1 (January 1977), pp. 54-73.

5. J.F. Rockart, "Chief Executives Define Their Own Data Needs," *Harvard Business Review*, Vol. 57, No. 2 (March-April 1979), pp. 81-93.

6. E. Chrysler, "Some Basic Determinants of Computer Programming Productivity," *Communications of the ACM*, Vol. 21, No. 6 (June 1978), pp. 472-83.

7. T. Gilb, *Software Metrics* (Cambridge, Mass.: Winthrop Publishers, 1977).

8. T. DeMarco, *Structured Analysis and System Specification* (New York: YOURDON Press, 1978).

9. H. Mintzberg, *The Nature of Managerial Work* (New York: Harper & Row, 1973).

10. P.G.W. Keen and M.S.S. Morton, *Decision Support Systems: An Organizational Perspective* (Reading, Mass.: Addison-Wesley, 1978).

11. L.H. Putnam and A. Fitzsimmons, "Estimating Software Costs," *Datamation* (three-part series): Vol. 25, No. 10 (September 1979), pp. 189-98; Vol. 25, No. 11 (October 1979), pp. 171-78; Vol. 25, No. 12 (November 1979), pp. 137-40.

12. G.M. Weinberg, *The Psychology of Computer Programming* (New York: Van Nostrand Reinhold, 1971).

13. E. Yourdon, *Structured Walkthroughs* (New York: YOURDON Press, 1978).

14. M.E. Fagan, "Design and Code Inspections to Reduce Errors in Program Development," *IBM Systems Journal,* Vol. 15, No. 3 (July 1976), pp. 182-211.

15. G.J. Myers, "A Controlled Experiment in Program Testing and Code Walkthroughs/Inspections," *Communications of the ACM,* Vol. 21, No. 9 (September 1978), pp. 760-68.

16. G.M. Weinberg, "Implementing Technical Reviews," *Ethnotechnical Review Handbook* (Lincoln, Neb.: Ethnotech, 3rd ed. draft, 1980).

6
Tying It
All Together

The team members take up the slack.

6
Tying It
All Together

"Let's not confuse the menu with the meal." —**Anonymous**

Throughout this book we have asserted that for any project to be completed successfully, a series of functions — normally considered management or leadership functions — must be performed. For these functions to be performed in a sensible, rational, and effective manner, the "right" information must be available for the "right" people to make the "right" regulatory decisions. What we have been arguing in this book is that, in most organizations, management's concern about power (that is, *who* makes the decisions), reward systems, and the responsibility for motivation can actually work *against* the successful completion of projects and the general level of job satisfaction and performance in project teams.*

We have also argued that as a result of these management attitudes, confusion exists in many projects between what is *project control* (keeping the project in control) and *management control* (keeping the programmers under control). Unless the two control systems are treated as separate elements, albeit with complex interactions, then the project management system, which enables decisions to be made about the project, can be overloaded by data received from the management control system.

---

*This conclusion is supported in a 1979 study by Joan Greenbaum of relations between data processing management and programmers [1]. "When I began this study, I examined management justifications for efficiency and tried to compare these to what was actually taking place in the work environment. The more I looked, the greater I found the differences between management and worker strategies for workplace activity."

■   A model of management and team functions

We are not advocating anarchy (although even that may provide a better environment than some we have observed), but rather that the functions essential for project management be "owned" and performed by the people best qualified to do them. These functions can be examined within the context of an integrated model of management and team functions within any organization. The model, shown in Fig. 6.1 and drawn from Constantine and Constantine [2], Mintzberg [3], and Beer [4], maps the spread of functions across the hierarchy of control levels and indicates the responsible area for each of the functions.

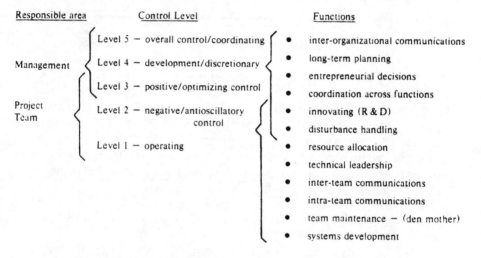

**Fig. 6.1. Integrated model of management and team functions
at various levels of control.**

As outlined in Chapter 3, the evidence from research into job redesign and enrichment programs and from research into the developments in socio-technical design (see Fig. 3.6) shows that the higher the level of team participation in what are traditionally considered to be management functions (that is, control levels three to five in Fig. 6.1), the greater the team's satisfaction and performance will become and the more management can concentrate on the critical higher control level functions over a longer time frame. Resource allocation; team maintenance; motivation and reward systems; development and entrepreneurial functions, such as evaluating new methods; tools and creative selection of tasks; and coordination of related work and liaison with other teams all can be done by team members in conjunction with some guidance from management. In the successful project teams that we have observed, this is the reality.

■ Form follows function

What is wrong with classic approaches to project management is exaggerated concern for the product. This preoccupation with form masks the need for management and teams to re-evaluate their methods of working, their views of control and responsibility, and their desired functions before any project control system can work.*

What we believe is that the structure of control implied in a project management system (form) reflects the organizational structure in which the system is used (function). *For a project management system to work, the organization must have a structure that works!* Our work with both large and small organizations has indicated that an organizational structure that is hierarchical and mechanical will also tend to have project management systems that are hierarchical and mechanistic. These hierarchically structured organizations are likely to have a long record of costly systems disasters — an indication that the structure and the resulting project control systems didn't work.

By contrast, an organizational structure that is leveled and dynamic will have leveled, dynamic project management systems. It is not surprising that organizations with such structures seem to have successful project histories.

■ Three critical factors

The shape, size, and structure of organizations that have successfully controlled projects with effectively working project management systems will obviously vary, but we can conclude that the nature of the three crucial factors in project management — management, teams, and project information systems — will be similar. Each factor is described below.

- Management is a group, usually of senior people, undertaking functions not involved in the day-to-day workings of the projects. These functions typically are concerned with dealing with corporate requirements; communicating with other companies, government, and other external groups; isolating critical success factors [7] that provide indications of the organization's

---

*The philosophy "form follows function," espoused in 1896 by architect Louis H. Sullivan [5], is reflected in the design work of Christopher Alexander, whose book *Notes on the Synthesis of Form* [6], which examines design from teapots to towns using high cohesion and low coupling concepts similar to those in structured design, had a significant influence on the structured methodologies.

health; and examining and selecting possible future directions for the company, determining within this corporate perspective the relative priorities of and resources for projects.

- Teams that work effectively *cannot* be labeled as egoless, hierarchical, or chief programmer/technical leader teams, because they must be flexible to shift from one type of team to another depending on the tasks to be performed. Such teams perform the optimizing functions of coordinating, scheduling, and monitoring tasks (both those within the team and related tasks from other groups). The teams are responsible for detecting and correcting minor fluctuations and for flagging major disruptions, providing possible solutions to management. They also handle the production of the system and work as a team to solve any personnel problems and take responsibility for the learning and growth of team members. These activities are handled within the team by the person best suited *at the time* to do them. The team's real leadership and structure will shift depending on the significant problem (technical, resource, or personnel) at that time. At one point in time, the team may appear to be a technical-leader team, but it may adapt to become a hierarchical or egoless team at other stages in the project.

- A project information system that channels information (not data) between management and teams links these two groups. The project information system includes the use of phased approaches and deliverables, or structured systems development methodologies, as the source not only for project status information but also as the proper method to build the system. The information is produced (and used by) the teams and management while they together perform the four processes of project management: work definition, planning, tracking, and reviewing. The project structure, process, and control are blended in an integrated unit with the system reporting on projects, not people.

■   **A summary of our guidelines**

To conclude, we come to reviewing our set of observations about and guidelines for successful project management developed in this and in the preceding five chapters of this book:

- The first step in achieving workable project management is to correctly draw the boundaries between the various people systems — users, management, and team — involved in the project and around the business system being developed.

- The second step is to ensure that project management systems act as information systems that enable communication between control and process systems.

- Third is for organizations to allow teams to evolve so as to allow team members to do what they do best, that is, to let teams evolve from their natural structure. Teams must be given adequate time and resources for learning and growth, and then be left alone to get on with the job of building systems.

- As outlined in Chapter 4, with the use of technical reviews and structured walkthroughs as reviewing processes, a systems development methodology approach must be implemented for project information systems.

- The theme of the fifth chapter is that teams must use the functions of work definition, planning, tracking, and reviewing to feed information back to management on project status.

- Finally, as outlined in this chapter, management and teams accepting joint responsibility for the project must recognize the functions they each are best equipped to do and must give each other the respect (authority, legitimacy) and support (resources, information) necessary to perform these functions.

These guidelines are drawn from our observations of real-world systems that are working in many different sizes and styles of organizations. The guidelines have evolved during long discussions with hundreds of project people, whose experiences, in the main, have been neither pleasant nor satisfying. What concerns us is that many of these people have worked in the prevailing classic project management systems environment, which appears to have made the project experience even less enjoyable. The project management system must help both the teams and their managers do their jobs better. You may feel that the only criteria worthy of consideration is that projects work on time and within budget, and that people's enjoyment of the project work is of secondary importance. *The overwhelming evidence does not support this view.* Our view is that if project members are given the responsibility and resources to manage their projects, we might see more projects that people enjoy working on and that work on time and within budget.

To summarize, we have found that people can and do work responsibly together to set goals, to determine policy, to deal with administrative details, to share information, to utilize a variety of organizational modes, and to handle the inevitable crises. Psychologist Carl Rogers described the process as follows: "The group is more capable of wise decisions than [is] one person, because it is calling on the leadership potentialities of all."*

---

*C. Rogers, *Carl Rogers on Personal Power* (New York: Delacorte Press, 1977), p. 104.

TEAM EXERCISE

Hollow Squares

This is a fun exercise that simulates the problem that occurs when management has the big picture but doesn't inform the team members about what is going on in the project (and vice versa).

○ Using the hollow square blueprint shown below, cut out of cardboard pieces to form the square. *Randomly* place the pieces in four envelopes labeled A, B, C, and D. Each piece will have two identifiers: its shape and its envelope label.

○ Select a management team and a project team, each having three to six people.

○ Give the management team the envelopes containing the random pieces and give them the hollow square blueprint.

○ Management has to instruct the project team on how to assemble the hollow square using the pieces in the envelopes. Management cannot show the team the blueprint and cannot alter or rearrange the contents of the envelopes. Management will have to describe pieces by their identifiers (for example, take the small square from envelope A and place it . . .).

○ Management must *complete* instructing the project team and must pass the envelopes to them in twenty-five minutes and cannot give more guidance after that time.

HOLLOW SQUARE BLUEPRINT

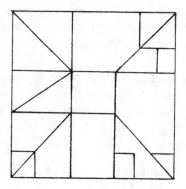

We have found that this exercise illustrates each of the three critical factors described in this chapter. Have fun — you'll probably be surprised at what happens.

References: Chapter 6

1. J.M. Greenbaum, *In the Name of Efficiency: Management Theory and Shopfloor Practice in Data-Processing Work* (Philadelphia: Temple University Press, 1979), p. 165.

2. L.L. and J.M. Constantine, *Group Marriage* (New York: Macmillan, 1973).

3. H. Mintzberg, *The Nature of Managerial Work* (New York: Harper & Row, 1973).

4. S. Beer, *The Heart of Enterprise* (New York: John Wiley & Sons, 1980).

5. L.H. Sullivan, "The Tall Office Building Artistically Considered," *Lippincott Magazine* (March 1896).

6. C. Alexander, *Notes on the Synthesis of Form* (Cambridge, Mass.: Harvard University Press, 1964).

7. J.F. Rockart, "Chief Executives Define Their Own Data Needs," *Harvard Business Review,* Vol. 57, No. 2 (March-April 1979), pp. 81-93.

7
Ideas for Action

Together the team members ensure that the dream comes true on time.

7
Ideas for Action

"There is no choice in the matter: You cannot sit and wait for things to come to you." —**Eldridge Cleaver***

Another facet of the paradox we mentioned at the beginning of this book is that *in many organizations, it is just as difficult to do something about project management as it is to do nothing.* A statement made by one of our seminar attendees, Roy Morian, upon returning to his organization points out how difficult the task of "doing something" is: "I went back with my eyes opened, but I still walked in darkness."

The dilemma, of course, partly results from uncertainty about responsibility and power in organizations, but it is also linked to the unwillingness of individuals to put themselves into a situation that involves risk, because they may try and fail. However, to paraphrase an old saying: "It is better to have tried and failed, than never to have tried at all." Moreover, we assume that the prospect of being involved in yet another project disaster, whose success you can do little to influence, is sufficient to make you believe that there *is* something you can do. One thing is fairly evident: Probably *no one else* is going to do much about the situation, especially management.

Constantine once asked in a seminar he was conducting, "Why does everyone want the answer?"[†] We could expand his question as follows: "Why does everyone want the answer but no one is willing to work hard to get it?" We believe that there are no white knights who will magically transform classical project management into workable project management. It is up to *you* — the project people and managers — to do something. After all, your job and esteem are affected by ineffective project management.

*E. Cleaver, *Soul on Ice* (London: Panther Books, 1972), p. 55.
[†]L. Constantine, "Structured Design," unpublished seminar notes, Melbourne, Australia, July 1976.

■ **Power and authority**

What can *you* do to change the way in which your project management functions? First, you must address the subjects of power and authority and freedom to innovate. Consider the system principle: *A couple is a triple,* which is a restatement of the system principle: *The whole is more than the sum of the parts* (Chapter 1).

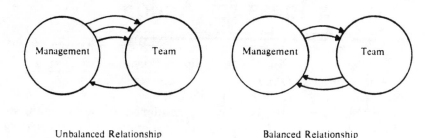

Unbalanced Relationship   Balanced Relationship

Fig. 7.1. A couple is a triple.

As shown in Fig. 7.1, the concept is that two components, say, management and team (the couple), work as a system only if the third component (the relationship between them) is functioning correctly — thus, the triple. Most contemporary models of power and authority relationships [1, 2, 3] suggest that in order for authority to exist within a system, the team must accept the authority that management exerts. Thus, power is a two-way path: the taking of power and the giving of power. The couple *is* a triple.

The first step (among many) in balancing a power relationship is to match the communication channels from manager to team, as in Fig. 7.1, with correspondingly strong lines from team to manager. For example, if management asks the team to release a member without a replacement, the team should calculate the impact of this loss in resources on schedules and other areas, and then ask management to choose which functions should be dropped or which deadlines should be altered as a result of management's decision. We believe that this use of information and feedback to management results in a more balanced and sensible power relationship.*

*If you are giving information to management and still hearing pathological responses like "work harder," then we suggest you join the twenty to thirty percent of computer people reported to be changing jobs each year.

■ **Force-field analysis**

A second possible method to use to improve project management is to use Lewin's force-field analysis model [1]. Using the model, as shown in Fig. 7.2, you can identify the forces and people in your work environment that move you toward change and those that work to prevent change. Lewin's technique is based on the fundamental idea that each of us exists amid positive and opposing forces, wherein the more we try to change things, the greater the strength of the opposing forces. Lewin's model enables the identification of the relative strengths of both sets of forces with the aid of a simple set of questions and of discussing your answers with people not involved directly in the issue.

Having identified the relative strengths of these forces, you can examine ways of *reducing* the strength of the opposing forces while *increasing* the strength of the positive forces. For example, you may be finding resistance to your efforts to implement structured analysis in your shop. By using Lewin's technique to analyze your situation, you may discover that the forces opposing this change are threefold: First, some of the "old-school" people may fear that they will lose technical superiority; second, you may lack money and resources to educate people; and third, you may have your own fears of failing. The forces supporting the change could be your (and your team's) desire to do things better — evidence that structured analysis works — and user demands for more involvement. Through discussion of supportive forces such as these, you can investigate and implement techniques to focus and use these positive forces while attempting to reduce the negative forces. We strongly urge you to investigate Lewin's technique. It works because it helps to clear your thoughts on your problem, and structures your attempts to solve it.

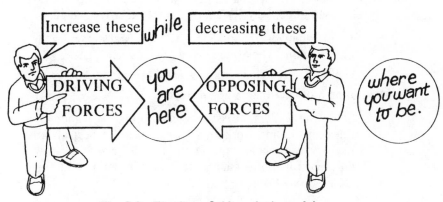

Fig. 7.2. The force-field analysis model.

■ Strategies for change

So far, so good. Both of these approaches — feedback to management and force-field analysis — require you to take responsibility for doing something about the situation. One of the most convenient reasons for not doing anything is "they"! In an internal IBM project management document, Metzger stated that "they" represent all upper levels of management and that we can't do anything unless "they" allow it [4]. However, Metzger claims there are innovators in every organization who are prepared to challenge and to change the rules of the system if they are no longer relevant. Moreover, we forget that for the people at levels under us, . . . we are "they." If you decide to challenge and change the rules, you may become a very isolated and lonely person. So, we want to leave you with some final ideas.

The first strategy involves judo. This Japanese martial art is based on the concept that you use your opponent's momentum and strength to your own advantage. The philosophy behind judo incorporates all the elements of Ashby's Law of Requisite Variety: If you want to change a system, you must have as much variety or modes of operating as the system has. You must understand how the structure works, how the power system works, and you must understand the people themselves who work to keep it as it is. Then, you don't take on the system head-on, but rather you use its rules and its strengths to change it.

We also consistently have found that in large organizations that require an increasing number of rules and regulations to maintain a stable state, the people who are responsible for these rules have difficulty understanding all their implications and possible interpretations. This leads to what we call "Rob's Paradox of Power": The bigger the organization and the more complex its rules, the more freedom you have for innovation.

Next, we leave you with a strategy (derived from Rowan [5]) that we have seen used effectively for gentle and productive change:

- Form a network of allies both inside and outside your organization who share your values and desire for change.

- Find a project that is about to start.

- Settle the leadership issue by examining the leadership roles and letting workers do what they are best at doing; try using role-duplication, that is, people sharing different functions, such as technical-leader and administrative functions, to gain flexibility.

- Inform the next higher level of management that you are trying something different but emphasize that it is not deviant or radical; if management agrees to let you change the status quo, great; if not, expect difficult times ahead. But if you have covered the previous three points, you should be able to persevere.

- Produce the desired result. This is the crucial step, for it will test the group's ability to work together and will provide you with back-up evidence and information in case management pressures you to conform.

- Expect top management's involvement. In most cases, your group, because it is different, will be treated as a special case, but because it is producing (and we would expect that it is producing very well), your group will be left alone, isolated, to prevent the spread of the "disease."

- Report on your progress to management. Identify and agree on new ways of working with middle management now that the new methods have proved successful for you.

- Help to spread your formula for success. Other groups and managers at your level will see the positive results and will want to join you; the organization will have begun to change from the bottom up.

■ Make your dreams come true on time

In our work with hundreds of project teams, we found many people who through their own sense of self-esteem put themselves at risk by using the guidelines to implement the approaches discussed in this book. The majority of *working* project management systems we observed had started at the team level first, then spread across the data processing organization. These successful systems helped the teams and management to make their dreams come true on time. Regardless of your level in the organization, *you can do it too!*

References: Chapter 7

1.   K. Lewin, "Frontiers in Group Dynamics," *Human Relations,* Vol. 1, No. 1 (1947), pp. 5-41.

2.   R. Emerson, "Power-Dependence Relations," *American Sociological Review,* Vol. 27 (1962), pp. 282-98.

3.   C. Cotten, "Measurement of Power-Balancing Styles and Some of Their Correlates," *Administrative Science Quarterly,* Vol. 21, No. 2 (June 1976), pp. 307-19.

4.   P. Metzger, *Programming Project Management Guide,* IBM Technical Report No. GA36-0005-1 (Gaithersburg, Md.: July 1974), p. 14-1.

5.   J. Rowan, *Ordinary Ecstasy* (London: Routledge & Kegan Paul, 1976), pp. 94-98.

Background Reading

Below are listed five books and one magazine article not usually listed as project management references, which we believe are essential reading for all project members. We have selected them because they are brief (most being fewer than 120 pages in length), inexpensive, and because we feel they provide a good, often unusual, background on project management issues. They should be purchased for each team as a project resource and be filed next to the team's slim volumes of structured system specification and project information reports.

Beer, Stafford. *Designing Freedom.* New York: John Wiley & Sons, 1974.

> This text contains transcripts of six radio broadcasts given by Beer in 1973 for the Canadian Broadcasting Corporation. It contains an overview of Beer's concepts and explains developments on Ross Ashby's initial work. It is a most lucid book on control, information, and freedom.

DeMarco, Tom. *Concise Notes on Software Engineering.* New York: YOURDON Press, 1979.

> This book provides a balanced, intelligent, state-of-the-art summary of the significant developments in the structured methodologies and in software engineering/metrics. It contains a superb bibliography.

Emery, Fred and Merrelyn. *Participative Design — Work and Community Life.* Canberra: Centre for Continuing Education, 1975.

> This provides a gentle and easy-to-read introduction to Fred Emery's work in developing alternative designs for groups and organizations, and his theoretical work in systems, which has altered the

working lives of many people for the better. In this seminal book, you can find a very clear description of semi-autonomous, multi-skilled teams and some practical hints.

Gall, John. *Systemantics.* New York: Pocket Books, 1978.

This delightful little book presents a set of axioms and laws for dealing with complex systems and their effects. The humorous and anecdotal style does not get in the way of Gall's very powerful insights.

Rowan, John. *Ordinary Ecstasy.* London: Routledge & Kegan Paul, 1976.

Organized in a very structured way, this book provides a brilliant integration of the various streams of contemporary psychology and sociology and serves not only as a great introduction to these topics, but also as a source book for further reading.

Canning, Richard, ed. "Project Management Systems," *EDP Analyzer,* Vol. 14, No. 9 (September 1976).

This overview of the practical experience of organizations with project management systems and of the lessons to be drawn from these is very comprehensive, and includes details of the essential functions of project management systems.

You don't have to take only our suggestions for what is essential reading. Slip away for an afternoon and browse through your organization's library, . . . you might be surprised at what you find there.

Bibliography

Alexander, C. *Notes on the Synthesis of Form.* Cambridge, Mass.: Harvard University Press, 1964.

American Federation of Information Processing Societies, Inc. *Proceedings of the 1977 National Computer Conference,* Vol. 46. Montvale, N.J.: AFIPS Press, 1977, pp. 255-59.

Argyris, C., and D.A. Schon. *Theory in Practice: Increasing Professional Effectiveness.* San Francisco: Jossey Bass, 1974.

Aron, J.D. "The Super-Programmer Project." *Software Engineering Techniques: Report on the 1969 Rome Conference,* eds. J.N. Buxton and B. Randell. Brussels, Belgium: NATO Science Committee, 1970.

Ashby, W.R. *Introduction to Cybernetics.* New York: John Wiley & Sons, 1961.

Baker, F.T., and H.D. Mills. "Chief Programmer Teams." *Datamation,* Vol. 19, No. 12 (December 1973), pp. 58-61.

Beer, S. *Designing Freedom.* New York: John Wiley & Sons, 1974.

————. *The Heart of Enterprise.* New York: John Wiley & Sons, 1980.

————. *Platform for Change.* New York: John Wiley & Sons, 1975.

Boehm, B.W. "Software Engineering — As It Is." *Proceedings of the Fourth International Conference on Software Engineering.* New York: Institute of Electrical and Electronics Engineers, 1979, pp. 11-21.

Brooks, F.P., Jr. *The Mythical Man-Month.* Reading, Mass.: Addison-Wesley, 1975.

Canning, R., ed. "The Production of Better Software." *EDP Analyzer,* Vol. 17, No. 2 (February 1979).

————. "Project Management Systems." *EDP Analyzer*, Vol. 14, No. 9 (September 1976).

————. "What Information Do Managers Need?" *EDP Analyzer*, Vol. 17, No. 6 (June 1979).

Cherns, A. "The Principles of Socio-technical Design." *Human Relations*, Vol. 29, No. 8 (1976), pp. 783-92.

Chrysler, E. "Some Basic Determinants of Computer Programming Productivity." *Communications of the ACM*, Vol. 21, No. 6 (June 1978), pp. 472-83.

Constantine, L.L., and J.M. Constantine. *Group Marriage*. New York: Macmillan, 1973.

Cotten, C. "Measurement of Power-Balancing Styles and Some of Their Correlates." *Administrative Science Quarterly*, Vol. 21, No. 2 (June 1976), pp. 307-19.

Couger, J.D., and R.A. Zawacki. "What Motivates DP Professionals?" *Datamation*, Vol. 24, No. 9 (September 1978), pp. 116-23.

Daly, E.B. "Organizing for Successful Software Development." *Datamation*, Vol. 25, No. 14 (December 1979), pp. 106-120.

David, E.E., Jr. "Design Criteria: Some Thoughts About Production of Large Software Systems." *Software Engineering: Report on a 1968 Conference in Garmisch*, eds. P. Naur and B. Randell. Brussels, Belgium: NATO Science Committee, 1969, p. 39.

Davis, L.E., and J.C. Taylor. *Design of Jobs*. New York: Penguin Books, 1972.

DeMarco, T. *Concise Notes on Software Engineering*. New York: YOURDON Press, 1979.

————. *Structured Analysis and System Specification*. New York: YOURDON Press, 1978.

Emerson, R. "Power-Dependence Relations." *American Sociological Review*, Vol. 27 (1962), pp. 282-98.

Emery, F.E., ed. *Systems Thinking*. Harmondsworth, Middlesex, England: Penguin Books, 1969.

————, and M. Emery. *Participative Design — Work and Community Life*. Canberra, ACT 2600, Australia: Centre for Continuing Education, Australian National University, P.O. Box 4 (1975).

Fagan, M.E. "Design and Code Inspections to Reduce Errors in Program Development." *IBM Systems Journal,* Vol. 15, No. 3 (July 1976), pp. 182-211.

Finkelstein, C. *Information Systems: The Challenge.* Seven Merriwa Street, Gordon, N.S.W. 2072, Australia: Infocom Monograph, 1979.

Flavin, M. *Fundamental Concepts of Information Modeling.* New York: YOURDON Press, prepublication draft, 1980.

Forbes, R. *Corporate Stress: How to Manage Stress and Make It Work for You.* New York: Doubleday, 1979.

Freedman, D., D. Gause, and G. Weinberg. "Organizing and Training for a New Software Development Project . . . That First Big Step." *Proceedings of the 1977 National Computer Conference,* Vol. 46. Montvale, N.J.: AFIPS Press, 1977, pp. 255-59.

Gall, J. *Systemantics.* New York: Pocket Books, 1978.

Gane, C., and T. Sarson. *Structured Systems Analysis: Tools and Techniques.* New York: Improved System Technologies, Inc., 1977.

Gilb, T. *Software Metrics.* Cambridge, Mass.: Winthrop Publishers, 1977.

Greenbaum, J.M. *In the Name of Efficiency: Management Theory and Shopfloor Practice in Data-Processing Work.* Philadelphia: Temple University Press, 1979.

Hackman, J.R., and E.E. Lawler. "Job Change and Motivation: A Conceptual Framework." *Design of Jobs,* eds. L.E. Davis and J.C. Taylor. New York: Penguin Books, 1972, pp. 75-84.

Hackman, J.R., and G. Oldham. "Development of the Job Diagnostic Survey." *Journal of Applied Psychology,* Vol. 60 (1975), pp. 159-70.

Hackman, J.R., G. Oldham, R. Janson, and K. Purdy. "A New Strategy for Job Enrichment." *California Management Review,* Vol. 17, No. 4 (1975), pp. 57-71.

Harman, W. "The Nature of Our Changing Society." *Management of Change and Conflict,* eds. J.M. Thomas and W. Bennis. Harmondsworth, Middlesex, England: Penguin Books, 1972, pp. 43-91.

Herzberg, F. *The Managerial Choice: To Be Efficient and to Be Human.* Homewood, Ill.: Dow Jones-Irwin, 1976.

Keen, P.G.W., and M.S.S. Morton. *Decision Support Systems: An Organizational Perspective.* Reading, Mass.: Addison-Wesley, 1978.

Keider, S.P. "Why Projects Fail." *Datamation,* Vol. 20, No. 12 (December 1974), pp. 53-55.

Kolence, K. "Production Control." Conference participant, *Software Engineering: Report on a 1968 Conference in Garmisch,* eds. P. Naur and B. Randell. Brussels, Belgium: NATO Science Committee, 1969, p. 87.

Lewin, K. "Frontiers in Group Dynamics." *Human Relations,* Vol. 1, No. 1 (1947), pp. 5-41.

Lientz, B.P., and E.B. Swanson. *Software Maintenance Management.* Reading, Mass.: Addison-Wesley, 1980.

————, and G.E. Tompkins. "Characteristics of Applications Software Maintenance." *Communications of the ACM,* Vol. 21, No. 6 (June 1978), pp. 466-71.

Maslow, A. *The Farther Reaches of Human Nature.* New York: Penguin Books, 1971.

McGregor, D. *The Human Side of Enterprise.* New York: McGraw-Hill, 1960.

Metzger, P. *Programming Project Management Guide.* IBM Technical Report No. GA36-0005-1 (Gaithersburg, Md.: July 1974).

Mintzberg, H. *The Nature of Managerial Work.* New York: Harper & Row, 1973.

Mumford, E. "Computer Systems and Work Design: Problems of Philosophy and Vision." *Personnel Review,* Vol. 3, No. 2 (Spring 1974), pp. 40-49.

————. "A Strategy for the Redesign of Work." *Personnel Review,* Vol. 5, No. 2 (Spring 1976), pp. 33-39.

Myers, G.J. "A Controlled Experiment in Program Testing and Code Walkthroughs/Inspections." *Communications of the ACM,* Vol. 21, No. 9 (September 1978), pp. 760-68.

Naur, P., and B. Randell, eds. *Software Engineering: Report on a 1968 Conference in Garmisch.* Brussels, Belgium: NATO Science Committee, 1969.

Nolan, R. "Managing the Crises in Data Processing." *Harvard Business Review,* Vol. 57, No. 2 (March-April 1979), pp. 115-26.

Peter, L.J., and R. Hull. *The Peter Principle: Why Things Go Wrong.* New York: William Morrow & Co., 1969.

Porter, L., and E.E. Lawler. "Antecedent Attitudes of Effective Management Performance." *Management and Motivation,* eds. V.H. Vroom and E.L. Deci. New York: Penguin Books, 1972, pp. 253-64.

Putnam, L.H., and A. Fitzsimmons. "Estimating Software Costs." *Datamation* (three-part series): Vol. 25, No. 10 (September 1979), pp. 189-98; Vol. 25, No. 11 (October 1979), pp. 171-78; Vol. 25, No. 12 (November 1979), pp. 137-40.

Rockart, J.F. "Chief Executives Define Their Own Data Needs." *Harvard Business Review,* Vol. 57, No. 2 (March-April 1979), pp. 81-93.

Rogers, C. *Carl Rogers on Personal Power.* New York: Delacorte Press, 1977.

Rowan, J. *Ordinary Ecstasy.* London: Routledge & Kegan Paul, 1976.

Sackman, H., W.J. Erikson, and E.E. Grant. "Exploratory Experimental Studies Comparing On-line and Off-line Programming Performance." *Communications of the ACM,* Vol. 11, No. 1 (January 1968), pp. 3-11.

Shannon, C.E., and W. Weaver. *The Mathematical Theory of Communication.* Urbana, Ill.: University of Illinois Press, 1949.

Selye, H. *The Stress of Life.* New York: McGraw-Hill, 1956.

Stevens, W., G. Myers, and L. Constantine. "Structured Design." *IBM Systems Journal,* Vol. 13, No. 2 (May 1974), pp. 115-39.

Sullivan, L.H. "The Tall Office Building Artistically Considered." *Lippincott Magazine* (March 1896).

Taylor, J. "The Human Side of Work: The Socio-Technical Approach to Work System Design." *Personnel Review,* Vol. 4, No. 3 (Summer 1975), pp. 17-22.

Thomas, J.M., and W. Bennis, eds. *The Management of Change and Conflict.* Harmondsworth, Middlesex, England: Penguin Books, 1972.

Vroom, V.H., and E.L. Deci, eds. *Management and Motivation.* New York: Penguin Books, 1972.

Walston, C.E., and C.P. Felix. "A Method of Programming Measurement and Estimation." *IBM Systems Journal,* Vol. 16, No. 1 (January 1977), pp. 54-73.

Weinberg, G.M. "Implementing Technical Reviews." *Ethnotechnical Review Handbook.* Lincoln, Neb.: Ethnotech, 3rd ed. draft, 1980.

―――. *An Introduction to General Systems Thinking.* New York: John Wiley & Sons, 1975.

―――. *The Psychology of Computer Programming.* New York: Van Nostrand Reinhold, 1971.

―――, and D. Weinberg. *On the Design of Stable Systems.* New York: John Wiley & Sons, 1980.

Yourdon, E. *A Methodology for Software Development.* New York: YOURDON Press, prepublication draft, 1979.

―――. *Structured Walkthroughs.* New York: YOURDON Press, 1978.

―――, ed. *Classics in Software Engineering.* New York: YOURDON Press, 1979.

―――, and L.L. Constantine. *Structured Design: Fundamentals of a Discipline of Computer Program and Systems Design.* New York: YOURDON Press, 1978.